Group
Treatment
of Adult
Incest
Survivors

Interpersonal Violence:
The Practice Series

Jon R. Conte, Series Editor

Interpersonal Violence: The Practice Series is devoted to mental health, social service, and allied professionals who confront daily the problem of interpersonal violence. It is hoped that the knowledge, professional experience, and high standards of practice offered by the authors of these volumes may lead to the end of interpersonal violence.

In this series...

Group
Treatment
of Adult
Incest
Survivors

MaryAnn Donaldson
Susan Cordes-Green

Interpersonal Violence:
The Practice Series

SAGE Publications
International Educational and Professional Publisher
Thousand Oaks   London   New Delhi

For information address:

SAGE Publications, Inc.
2455 Teller Road
Thousand Oaks, California 91320

SAGE Publications Ltd.
6 Bonhill Street
London EC2A 4PU
United Kingdom

SAGE Publications India Pvt. Ltd.
M-32 Market
Greater Kailash I
New Delhi 110 048 India

Printed in the United States of America

Library of Congress Cataloging-in-Publication Data

Donaldson, Mary Ann.
    Group treatment of adult incest survivors / Mary Ann Donaldson, Susan Cordes-Green.
        p. cm.   —   (Interpersonal violence ; the practice series: 5)
    Includes bibliographical references and index.
    ISBN 0-8039-6165-0.   —   ISBN 0-8039-6166-9 (pbk.)
    1. Incest victims—Rehabilitation. 2. Group psychotherapy.
3. Adult child sexual abuse victims—Rehabilitation. I. Cordes-Green, Susan. II. Title. III. Series: Interpersonal violence.
RC560.I53D66 1994
616.85'83690651—dc20   94-6852

94 95 96 97 98 10 9 8 7 6 5 4 3 2

Sage Production Editor: Diana E. Axelsen

Contents

Acknowledgment

Preparation of this book was supported by the Alliance for Sexual Abuse Prevention and Treatment. The Alliance is a conjoint training program of the North Dakota Department of Human Services and the Village Family Service Center.

Preface

❏ Overview of the Village Family Service Center's Incest Treatment Program

History. During the late 1970s and early 1980s, Mary Ann Donaldson began treating adult incest survivors (many referred from a local rape crisis center) who were experiencing symptoms that included anxiety, depression, flashbacks, and nightmares. She consulted with an area psychiatrist who had been working with post-traumatic stress disorder (PTSD); the results of their research (Donaldson & Gardner, 1985) suggested that the PTSD diagnosis is appropriate for many survivors of incest who are troubled enough to seek a treatment program.

At first, all clients were seen on an individual basis, but as the numbers grew, groups were formed and more therapists were recruited to become part of a treatment team. The earliest groups, which were semistructured and topic centered, lasted about 12 weeks. As the literature and therapists' practical understanding regarding the consequences of incest grew, they began to see a need for longer group experiences. Clients and therapists alike felt that short-term group was, in many cases, insufficient to deal with family systems issues, individual developmental processes, grief, assertion, and the like. The current program is the result of attempts to meet a wide range of needs while allowing individual choices.

Current program. The goal of the Village's incest treatment program is to provide change-oriented therapy in a supportive context. We believe that our clients benefit most when they are able to understand their victimization as an abuse of power and a denial of personal rights on the cultural as well as the familial level. Therefore, we view our clients as active partners in their treatment process.

Our program serves 50 to 70 adult female survivors at a given time. On the average, clients participate in our program for about one year. Over the years, we have worked with nearly 500 incest clients. According to a study of 104 of our clients (Edwards & Donaldson, 1989), survivors ranged in age from 17 to 54, with an average age of 28. Nearly 30% of the subjects were married and 30% were separated or divorced; the rest had never married. Nearly 80% had a high school education and 15% had attended college. Sixty percent reported middle to low incomes and 34% received some sort of financial assistance.

Our present treatment team consists of five therapists, all of whom work with the program part time. Therapists who conduct our groups have a minimum of masters' level training in programs such as clinical social work, psychology, counseling, family therapy, and psychiatric nursing.

Following is an overview of the components in our current treatment package. All components are discussed in greater detail in this book.

- Individual therapy and assessment: Individual therapy is provided for an average of 5 sessions before a client is referred to the group component.
- Education groups: Education groups precede the therapy groups and are conducted over 4 sessions.

- Pretherapy groups: Those clients who complete the education groups and want to enter a therapy group must first complete 3 to 4 pregroup orientation sessions.
- Therapy groups: Clients who enter group therapy commit for 6-month segments. The groups consist of six to eight members who meet for 1 ½ hours in weekly sessions.

Referrals or supplemental in-house services are provided for additional diagnoses, marital and sex therapy, and parenting. Spouses of our clients may participate in a partners group that is led by a member of the treatment team and a male staff cotherapist. Clients may also be referred to a local self-help support group, usually when they are "advanced" or their program is completed.

1

Overview—
Incest Survivors
and Group Treatment

Group therapy is a widely used and accepted form of intervention that has been applied to a variety of problems and populations. Proponents of the group process list numerous benefits for clients and practitioners alike. Groups tend to be cost-effective, and they allow more people access to programs, provide greater support for members, facilitate the practice of new skills and behaviors, and provide a social milieu in which individuals can work through problems that occurred in social settings (Corey, 1985). Yalom (1985) lists 11 therapeutic factors that result from participation in the group process: instillation of hope, universality, imparting of information, altruism, the corrective recapitulation of primary family group, development of socializing techniques, imitative behavior, catharsis, interpersonal learning, group cohesiveness, and existential factors.

These therapeutic factors may be of particular benefit in ameliorating symptoms experienced by adult survivors of childhood incest
(Courtois, 1988; Forward & Buck, 1978). To discuss the application
of group therapy to this population, we must first review the available research literature that addresses the possible sequelae of this
type of abuse.

❑ Long-Term Effects
of Childhood Sexual Abuse

Surveys of women in general population samples estimate overall
prevalence rates of childhood sexual abuse (CSA) at around 20-40%
(Finkelhor, 1979; Finkelhor, Hotaling, Lewis, & Smith, 1990; Russell,
1986). However, rates vary from 6.8% (Stein, Golding, Siegel, Burnam,
& Sorenson, 1988) to 60% (Peters, 1988). Variations in results may be
attributed to differences in definitions of abuse, sampling, sample
size, or methods of obtaining retrospective data.

Adult women who report a history of CSA, including incestuous
abuse, share a variety of problems and characteristics that are assumed to be linked to their earlier abusive experiences (Briere, 1992a;
Browne & Finkelhor, 1986; Courtois, 1988; Herman, 1981; Tsai &
Wagner, 1978). Finkelhor and Browne (1985) theorize that the deleterious effects of CSA are the result of traumagenic factors that were
manifested within the abusive relationship. These include traumatic
sexualization, betrayal, powerlessness, and stigmatization. Other
researchers attribute the negative effects of CSA to cognitive distortions (Celano, 1992; Gold, 1986; Harter, Alexander, & Neimeyer, 1988;
Jehu, 1988), psychological defenses (Blake-White & Kline, 1985;
Courtois, 1988; Summit, 1983), learning history (Jehu, 1988), altered
or truncated development (Alexander, 1992a; Meiselman 1978), factors in the family environment (Alexander, 1985; Conte & Schuerman,
1987; Edwards & Alexander, 1992; Madonna, Van Scoyk, & Jones,
1991), emotional abuse integral to the sexual abuse (Briere, 1992a),
and socio-cultural factors (Brickman, 1984; Finkelhor, 1984, Yassen
& Glass, 1984).

For the purpose of a brief review of the research literature address-ing the sequelae of incest and other CSA, we will consider the follow-ing categories of problems, symptoms, and characteristics: emo-tional and cognitive effects, social and interpersonal functioning, physical and sexual functioning, compulsive behaviors and behaviors of excess, and psychiatric diagnoses.

EMOTIONAL AND COGNITIVE EFFECTS

Anxiety and Tension

Various features of anxiety, such as tension, hyper-alertness, fears and worries, a sense of powerlessness in the face of perceived or impending danger, and related autonomic arousal, seem to be con-nected with early sexual abuse experiences (Briere, 1989). In both clinical and nonclinical samples, women reporting CSA, as compared to those reporting none, have been found to have greater levels of anxiety or tension (Briere & Runtz, 1988a, 1988b; Bryer, Nelson, Miller, & Krol, 1987; Bushnell, Wells, & Oakley-Browne, 1992; Courtois, 1988; Gelinas, 1983; Lundberg-Love, Marmion, Ford, Geffner, & Peacock, 1992; Murphy et al., 1988; Sedney & Brooks, 1984; Stein et al., 1988). Studies have also found that abuse survivors experience higher levels of other emotions that may be linked to anxiety, including anger control problems (Briere & Runtz, 1988b; Murphy et al., 1988), mania (Bushnell et al., 1992), fear of being alone (Stein et al., 1988), sleep disturbances (Sedney & Brooks, 1984), flashbacks and nightmares (Donaldson & Gardner, 1985), and recurrent thoughts and images related to abuse (Gelinas, 1983). Victims of parental incest, those abused for a longer duration, and those abused by an older offender tend to report the greatest levels of anxiety (Briere & Runtz, 1988a).

Depression

Depression is a frequently noted, often chronic symptom that may be evidenced in suicidal or self-destructive behaviors (Courtois, 1988). Studies assessing depressive symptomatology in nonclinical samples suggest that women sexually abused as children experience greater levels of depression and other mood disturbances than do nonabused subjects (Briere & Runtz, 1988a; Bushnell et al., 1992; Gold, 1986; Lundberg-Love et al., 1992; Sedney & Brooks, 1984; Stein et al., 1988). Studies that involve clinical samples also note elevated levels of depression in women sexually abused as children (Bryer et al., 1987; Jackson, Calhoun, Amick, Maddever, & Habif, 1990; Jehu, 1988; Kinzl & Biebl, 1991). Browne and Finkelhor (1986), however, note that such findings are inconsistent, especially in studies involving clinical comparison samples (e.g., Herman, 1981; Meiselman, 1978). This inconsistency may be explained by the fact that clinical subjects, in general, are likely to experience high levels of depression (Lehman, 1985; Millon & Kotik, 1985). For incest survivors, depressive symptoms may be related to powerlessness (Finkelhor & Browne, 1985), to negative thoughts and beliefs (Jehu, 1988), or to grief resulting from a loss of normalcy or safety (Courtois & Watts, 1982; Hays, 1985).

Guilt and Shame

Descriptions of incest survivors consistently note that they report feeling guilt and shame regarding their abuse experiences (Browne & Finkelhor, 1986; Courtois, 1988; Tsai & Wagner, 1978). Guilt and shame may be mediated by internal attributions of responsibility that lead to self-blame (Celano, 1992). Jehu's (1988) assessment of women presenting for treatment for CSA indicated that 88% felt guilty about the abuse. Several prevalent beliefs were associated with guilt: distorted beliefs about compliance with the perpetrator, participation in the maintenance of secrecy, seductive behaviors, curiosity about sex, experience of physical and emotional pleasure in the abusive situation, and material rewards gained through the abuse. Similar results, also with clinical samples, are reported by Kinzl and Biebl (1991). Stein et al. (1988), using a nonclinical sample, likewise note that abused women, as compared to nonabused women, reported significantly higher levels of guilt and shame.

Low Self-Esteem/
Distorted Self-Perceptions

Descriptions of CSA survivors indicate that they tend to experience low or unstable self-esteem (Browne & Finkelhor, 1986; Courtois,

1988; Gold, 1986; Herman, 1981; Jackson et al., 1990; Jehu, 1988; Kinzl & Biebl, 1991; Tsai & Wagner, 1978; Van Buskirk & Cole, 1983). Adult survivors frequently describe themselves as "different" from other people (Harter et al., 1988; Jehu, 1988) or as feeling stigmatized by their early experiences (Browne & Finkelhor, 1986). Low self-esteem may also relate to reported distortions in body image (Jackson et al., 1990; Sullivan, 1988).

Low self-esteem and negative self-evaluation may be induced or exacerbated by the victim's assumptions of guilt and responsibility (Briere, 1989). Gold (1986) reports that women in a nonclinical sample who were sexually abused in childhood and who displayed both psychological distress and low self-esteem characteristically made stable internal and global attributions regarding negative events. It is not clear whether the abuse alone causes negative self-perceptions or this type of attributional style, or whether it serves to intensify them.

SOCIAL AND INTERPERSONAL FUNCTIONING

Interpersonal Difficulties

Women with a CSA history may also have difficulties with interpersonal relationships and social adjustment, and they may report heightened interpersonal sensitivity (Alter-Reid, Gibbs, Lachenmeyer, Sigal, & Masseth, 1986; Browne & Finkelhor, 1986; Harter et al., 1988; Murphy et al., 1988; Van Buskirk & Cole, 1983). Jehu (1988) organizes various interpersonal problems into four common themes: isolation, insecurity, discord, and inadequacy.

Increased social isolation (or perception of social isolation) is an effect discussed both in descriptions of CSA victims and in comparisons of abused with nonabused subjects (Briere & Runtz, 1988b; Harter et al., 1988; Jehu, 1988; Tsai & Wagner, 1978). Insecurity may stem from experiences of betrayal and powerlessness that result in fear or mistrust in relationships (Briere, 1989, 1992b; Browne & Finkelhor, 1986; Gelinas, 1983; Herman, 1981; Jehu, 1988; Tsai & Wagner, 1978). Jehu (1988) determined that 88% of his clinical sample reported feeling insecure in relationships. Adult abuse survivors also report a high rate of discord or disruption in intimate relationships. In Jehu's

(1988) clinical sample, every subject in a committed relationship reported that it was troubled. High levels of marital problems have
also been reported by Herman (1981) and Meiselman (1978). Part-
nership discord may be related to issues such as mistrust or betrayal
(Courtois, 1988), to abuse survivors' tendency to be adversarial and
manipulative in relationships (Briere, 1989), to insecure attachments
(Alexander, 1992), and to the presence of sexual dysfunctions (Briere,
1989, 1992a). Finally, social difficulties may derive from inadequacy
in social skills, particularly a lack of assertion (Jehu, 1988; Tsai &
Wagner, 1978; Van Buskirk & Cole, 1983).

Although many types of social functioning problems are reported,
few have been the subject of controlled, nonclinical studies. One
exception (Harter et al., 1988) found in a college student sample that
abused students had lower ratings than nonabused students on
social adjustment measures, but did not report evidence of generalized social fragmentation in their lives.

Revictimization

Numerous studies note that CSA victims are vulnerable to subsequent victimizations including rape, physical assault, domestic
violence, and emotional abuse (Briere & Runtz, 1986; Browne &
Finkelhor, 1986; Goodwin, Cheeves, & Connell, 1990; Jackson et al.,
1990; Miller, Moeller, Kaufman, DiVasto, Pathak, & Christy, 1978;
Wyatt, Guthrie, & Notgrass, 1992). Wyatt et al. (1992) observe that
there is considerable variation in the methodologies involved in
these studies and that few studies have examined the differential
effects of type of abuse, age of first abuse, or type of revictimization.

In a study that did address differential effects, Wyatt et al. (1992)
found that women sexually abused in childhood are 2.4 times more
likely to be revictimized than nonabused women. Women with two
or more childhood victimizations reported the highest rate of un-
wanted pregnancies and a higher rate of sexual involvements. Briere
and Runtz (1986) found similar rates of adult rapes in their sample
and a significantly higher incidence of battery in adult relationships.

Several studies suggest that incestuous abuse may have a more
profound effect on revictimization than nonincestuous abuse. Miller

et al. (1978) determined that adult victims of multiple sexual assaults (as compared to single assaults) were more likely to have been incest victims and had a greater incidence of general psychological problems.

Revictimization is considered to be related to helplessness and powerlessness (Briere, 1992a), perceived vulnerability (Marhoefer-Dvorak, Resick, Hutter, & Girelli, 1988), low self-esteem, a failure to have learned personal boundaries (Briere, 1992a), exaggerated gender roles (Maltz & Holman, 1987), and features of post-traumatic stress disorder (Coons, Bowman, Pellow, & Schneider, 1989).

PHYSICAL AND SEXUAL FUNCTIONING

Sexual Difficulties

Numerous anecdotal and empirical reports of CSA survivors describe a variety of adult sexual problems (Briere, 1992a; Browne & Finkelhor, 1986; Finkelhor, Hotaling, Lewis, & Smith, 1989; Gelinas, 1983; Jehu, 1988; Meiselman, 1978; Saunders, Villeponteaux, Lipovsky, Kilpatrick, & Veronen, 1992; Tsai & Wagner, 1978; Van Buskirk & Cole, 1983). Common sexual problems include: sexual fears or phobia, decreased sexual desire, arousal dysfunction, general sexual dissatisfaction, and orgasmic and intromission problems (Becker, Skinner, Abel, & Cichon, 1986; Douglas, Matson, & Hunter, 1989; Jackson et al., 1990; Jehu, 1988; Maltz & Holman, 1987; Rowe & Savage, 1988; Tsai, Feldman-Summers, & Edgar, 1979).

These sexual problems appear to be greatly overrepresented in this population. Clinical studies find very high rates of sexual problems in CSA/incest survivors receiving treatment for abuse effects (94%, Jehu, 1988) or for other diagnoses (90%, Kinzl & Biebl, 1991). Samples of nonclinical populations report somewhat lower (but still elevated) rates of sexual dysfunctions (e.g., 58.6%, Becker et al., 1986; 65%, Jackson et al., 1990). Studies comparing CSA survivors and nonabused subjects in clinical and nonclinical samples indicate that abused subjects are two or three times more likely to have experienced sexual problems (Briere & Runtz, 1988b; Meiselman, 1978; Pribor & Dinwiddie, 1992; Saunders et al., 1992).

Because sexual problems are a logical consequence of sexual abuse, neither the high rate nor the variety of sexual problems experienced by this population is surprising. Several different etiologic explanations are offered. Phobic or avoidant sexual difficulties may be attributed directly to responses, such as flashbacks or anxiety attacks, which were conditioned in the abusive experience (Douglas et al., 1989; Jehu, 1988; Maltz & Holman, 1987). Other problems and behaviors may be mediated by beliefs or emotions stemming from the abuse, the family environment, or the culture. For example, beliefs about culpability may mediate fear and anxiety regarding sexuality (Rowe & Savage, 1988).

Somatization

As Briere and Runtz (1988a) observe, despite the conceptual link between anxiety and sexual trauma with physical problems or preoccupation, the earliest literature of the long-term effects of CSA generally did not address the presence of somatic complaints in this population. Recent studies have linked a history of CSA with a variety of physical complaints, including many possibly related to chronic anxiety, such as headaches, insomnia, muscle tension and spasms, or gastrointestinal disturbances (Briere, 1992a; Courtois, 1988; Cunningham, Pearce, & Pearce, 1988; Drossman et al., 1990). One of the more frequently noted physical problems for this group has been chronic pelvic pain (Gross, Doerr, Caldirola, Guzinski, & Ripley, 1980-81; Walker et al., 1988; Walker, Katon, Neraas, Jemelka, & Massoth, 1992).

Studies using both clinical and nonclinical samples have found an association between a CSA history and higher overall levels of somatization (Briere & Runtz, 1988a; Bryer et al., 1987; Bushnell et al., 1992; Walker et al., 1988; Walker et al., 1992). Evidence suggests that somatization is associated with high levels of dissociation (Chu & Dill, 1990) and may be particularly pronounced when the sexual abuse was intrafamilial (Briere & Runtz, 1988a; Bushnell et al., 1992; Lundberg-Love et al., 1992) or if the perpetrator was significantly older or used force (Briere & Runtz, 1988a).

COMPULSIVE BEHAVIORS
AND BEHAVIORS OF EXCESS

Substance Abuse

For survivors of abuse, substance use may allow avoidance of painful memories by providing anesthesia (Briere, 1992a; Root, 1989). A history of CSA may also increase the potential of relapse in recovering substance abusers (Hurley, 1990; Young, 1990). Research that explores the connection between CSA/incest and subsequent substance abuse approaches the issue from two directions: the rate of CSA history among adult substance abusers and the rate of substance abuses among adults reporting a CSA history.

Assessments of women undergoing treatment for substance abuse find high rates of CSA in these populations (Ladwig & Anderson, 1989; Root, 1989). Swett, Cohen, Surrey, Compaine, and Chavez (1991), in a study involving 189 clinic outpatients not admitted for alcohol abuse, found the highest rate of alcohol abuse among those who had experienced both physical and sexual abuse in childhood, and the lowest rate among those who had experienced neither form of abuse. Overall, the alcohol abuse rate for the group that had suffered one or both forms of childhood abuse, as compared to the nonabused group, was double. These authors hypothesize that patterns of abuse for many are in some way linked to a family member's alcohol use. Other clinical studies (Brown & Anderson, 1991; Pribor & Dinwiddie, 1992; Singer, Petchers, & Hussey, 1989) have found similar rates of alcohol use and dependence in subjects with CSA histories.

In a large nonclinical sample, Stein et al. (1988) found that subjects with a CSA history reported higher rates of substance abuse (over two times), alcohol abuse or dependence (two times) and drug abuse or dependence (almost five times) than did the nonabused group. Briere and Runtz (1988b) and Peters (1988) report similar results.

Eating Disorders

The notion that eating disorders are in some way linked to CSA experiences has received considerable attention. Survivors of CSA and clients with eating disorders may share issues regarding powerlessness, control, low self-esteem, perfectionism, and distrust of perceptions, as well as denial, repression, or shame regarding sexuality (Kearney-Cooke, 1988; Oppenheimer, Howells, Palmer, & Chaloner, 1985; Sloan & Leichner, 1986). Scott and Thoner (1986) found that anorexics and incest survivors displayed similar personality profiles. Furthermore, Root and Fallon (1989) suggest that PTSD symptoms parallel critical features of bulimia.

However, although the features of eating disorders seem intuitively to be linked to the psychological sequelae of incest, the empirical literature on this subject has yielded equivocal and somewhat confusing results. A number of studies involving clients with either anorexia and/or bulimia (Bulik, Sullivan, & Rorty, 1989; Hall, Tice, Beresford, Wooley, & Hall, 1989; Kearney-Cooke, 1988; Oppenheimer et al., 1985; Root & Fallon, 1988) assessed high rates of CSA in their samples. Of these, only the Hall et al. (1989) study utilized a control group. However, Beckman and Burns (1990), in a controlled study with a nonclinical population, did not find a higher rate of CSA in subjects who were bulimic. Pope and Hudson (1992), in a review of both controlled and uncontrolled retrospective studies, suggest that once methodological differences are accounted for, rates of sexual abuse histories in bulimia populations are comparable to those found in the general population.

Pribor and Dinwiddie (1992) found that incest victims in treatment were significantly more likely than nonabused controls to meet diagnostic criteria for bulimia. However, in a clinical sample, Finn, Hartman, Leon, and Lawson (1986) failed to find any differences on an assessment of disordered eating between women with a history of CSA and those reporting none. Palmer and Oppenheimer (1992), in comparing rates of eating disorders and other diagnoses among subjects who had experienced CSA, found no special association between abuse and eating disorders.

A number of studies that failed to find a direct link between CSA and eating disorders have noted some interesting relationships. Waller (1992) determined that increased bingeing and vomiting were associated with familial abuse; bingeing was associated with an onset of abuse at a younger age. Calam and Slade (1989) found that the use of force during abuse predicted higher symptomatology in general, dieting and anorexia in specific. Smolak, Levine, and Sullens (1990) discovered a strong link between eating disturbances and family factors, particularly a lack of family support. This was especially pronounced for CSA victims. Steiger and Zanko (1990) note that abuse-related trauma seemed to be strongly associated with bulimic factors. They speculate that this may be a function of family characteristics shared by both groups. Wonderlich et al. (1992), in a controlled study of 50 clients in the Village's treatment program, determined that incest was associated with disturbed eating behaviors and bulimic-type symptoms.

Connors and Morse (1993), in a review of the literature that addresses the link between CSA and eating disorders, conclude that, although CSA alone cannot be assumed to cause an eating disorder directly, it may well be an important risk factor. Future research must continue to address the complex interactions and specific risk factors that both sexual abuse and eating disorders may share.

Self-Destructive Behaviors

The literature addressing the long-term effects of CSA consistently notes, in both clinical and nonclinical samples, a link between the childhood trauma and various types of self-destructive behavior or desires in later life (Briere & Runtz, 1987, 1988b; Brown & Anderson, 1991; Browne & Finkelhor, 1986; Kinzl & Biebl, 1991; Saunders et al., 1992; Shapiro, 1987; van der Kolk, Perry, & Herman, 1991). Self-destructive behaviors may allow a cathartic release of inner emotions (de Young, 1982; Wise, 1989), may restore defenses (de Young, 1982), or may serve as a form of self-punishment because of self-blame (Shapiro, 1987).

The work of van der Kolk et al. (1991) suggest that these behaviors are maintained by a lack of secure attachments. If this is indeed the case, one might expect that incest victims would display these behaviors to a greater degree than victims of nonfamilial sexual abuse. Carroll, Schaffer, Spensley, and Abramowitz (1980) found in their samples that the highest degree of adult self-mutilation was associated with childhood sexual activity with older male relatives.

PSYCHIATRIC DIAGNOSES

The presence of a history of incest or CSA is frequently first identified when a patient presents with other types of psychiatric symptoms or diagnoses (Jacobson & Herald, 1990; Lundberg-Love et al., 1992). Clinical studies that investigate CSA histories indicate a high prevalence rate among female psychiatric inpatients (Bryer et al., 1987; Jacobson & Herald, 1990; Rosenfeld, 1979) and also a high rate of a number of psychiatric disorders among incest survivors receiving treatment for the abuse (Pribor & Dinwiddie, 1992).

Research utilizing nonclinical samples has found similar relationships. In comparing subjects with abuse histories with nonabused subjects, Stein et al. (1988) found abused subjects more likely to have a psychiatric diagnosis. Briere and Runtz (1988b) determined that abused subjects were more likely to have had at least one psychiatric hospitalization than nonabused subjects, and Jackson et al. (1990) found abused subjects more likely to have undergone psychiatric treatment.

Personality Disorders

Both clinical and nonclinical studies have found a higher rate of personality disorders in CSA victims than in nonvictimized adults (Brown & Anderson, 1991; Stein et al., 1988). Most of these studies have addressed either borderline personality disorder (BPD) or multiple personality disorder (MPD).

Borderline personality disorder. Several studies report that women diagnosed with BPD relate extraordinarily high rates of a childhood history of incest or other sexual abuse (Barnard & Hirsch, 1985; Herman, Perry, & van der Kolk, 1989; Ogata et al., 1990). Conversely, psychiatric patients with a history of sexual abuse have been found to have higher rates of BPD (Brown & Anderson, 1991: Bryer et al., 1987; Goodwin, Cheeves, & Connell, 1990) or symptom clusters related to the significant features of BPD (Nigg et al., 1991). Higher rates of both incest and BPD have also been reported to occur in medical patients complaining of chronic pelvic pain (Gross et al., 1980-81).

The etiology of BPD assumes that it results from some form of disruption in development. Briere (1989) suggests that the genesis of BPD may be attributed to severe emotional abuse that is concurrent with sexual abuse and that results in characteristic cognitive, emotional, and social patterns. In looking at such patterns, Nigg et al. (1991) analyzed the early memories of victims and discovered that they chose memories that reflected specific personal and interpersonal schemas, especially malevolent representations, which may have played a role in the development of BPD. Herman et al. (1989) posit that, although child abuse alone may be insufficient to cause BPD, it may be a vital factor. They speculate that BPD may be a special form of post-traumatic stress disorder (PTSD), and add that BPD-like symptoms often seem to ameliorate when the abuse trauma is addressed.

MPD and dissociative experiences. Dissociative symptoms or experiences such as "spacing out," losing time, derealization, or out-of-body experiences are found to be fairly common among adults who experienced CSA (Blake-White & Kline, 1985; Briere & Runtz, 1988a, 1988b; Chu & Dill, 1990; Herman & Schatzow, 1984; Waller et al., 1988, 1992). Blake-White and Kline (1985) view dissociation as stemming from the abused child's intense need to repress overwhelming emotions. Dissociation subsequently becomes a learned behavior in response to pain and possibly an essential facet of the victim's behavioral repertoire and personality (Summit, 1988). Dissociative responding, in its most extreme form, may result in MPD (Putnam, 1989; Summit, 1988). Several studies support this theory, suggesting that a strong link exists between MPD and a history of CSA. Coons and Milstein (1986) determined that 15 of 20 patients with MPD had experienced CSA. Putnam, Guroff, Silberman, Barban, and Post (1986) found that 97% of their MPD patients had experienced some form of childhood abuse, 83% had been sexually abused, and 63% had experienced incest. Similar results were reported by Ross et al., (1991). Although one would assume that more severe types of abuse would lead to more dissociation and subsequently to MPD, the specific circumstances most likely to result in these coping patterns remain to be determined.

Affective Disorders

CSA may also be linked with adult affective disorders. Pribor and Dinwiddie (1992) diagnosed a higher rate of major depression among clinical patients in an incest-history group than in a comparison group. Several large-scale nonclinical studies (Peters, 1988; Saunders et al., 1992; Stein et al., 1988) found higher rates of affective disorders, particularly major depression, in adult survivors of childhood sexual abuse than in nonabused participants. Peters (1988) found that the prevalence of major depression was correlated with a history of contact sexual abuse, but not noncontact abuse (i.e., exposure or innuendo). As was discussed earlier, the presence of affective disorders in abuse survivors may be attributed to a variety of factors.

Anxiety Disorders/PTSD

Adults with a history of CSA, in both clinical and nonclinical samples, have been found to experience higher rates of anxiety disorders than nonabused subjects (Kinzl & Biebl, 1991; Pribor & Dinwiddie, 1992; Stein et al., 1988). Specific anxiety disorders found to be prevalent in this group include agoraphobia, social phobia, panic disorder, and obsessive/compulsive disorder (Saunders et al., 1992). However, the greatest emphasis has been placed on the particularly high incidence of PTSD attributed to this population.

An earlier study involving clients in the Village's incest treatment program (Donaldson & Gardner, 1985) found that 25 of the 26 clients met the DSM III (APA, 1980) diagnostic criteria for PTSD. Similar results were reported by Lindberg and Distad (1985). Both studies involved survivors who had sought treatment; neither used appropriate control groups. Coons et al. (1989), in a study comparing patients sexually abused in childhood to female bulimics, found a much higher incidence of PTSD-related symptomatology and dissociation in the abused group.

However, in a large nonclinical, nonstudent sample, Greenwald and Leitenberg (1990) found that only 17% of subjects who reported CSA met the diagnostic criteria for PTSD. They noted that the PTSD symptoms were most severe in victims of father/daughter incest and/or incest involving completed intercourse. Saunders et al. (1992) similarly found that subjects who were raped or molested in childhood were more likely to have experienced PTSD than were victims of noncontact sexual abuse. Taken together, the studies suggest that victims who seek therapy may be more likely to be suffering from PTSD than those who do not; moreover, factors associated with the abusive experience may influence the subsequent development of PTSD.

Concepts inherent in the etiology of PTSD, such as recall and reactualization of traumatic experiences, seem to be particularly applicable to victims of CSA (Kinzl & Biebl, 1991). Furthermore, many of the postabuse symptoms experienced by victims of CSA, including flashbacks, sleep disturbances and nightmares, anxiety, and dissociation, meet the criteria for PTSD (Briere & Runtz, 1988b).

Finkelhor (1987, 1990) argues that the PTSD conceptualization is limited and overemphasizes emotional consequences, that research on CSA/PTSD lacks empirical integrity, and that this syndrome does not explain the impact of abuse on those who do not develop PTSD-like symptoms. He adds that PTSD theory often does not fit abusive experiences and does not account for other factors in the abusive situation.

EFFECTS AND SUBPOPULATIONS

Descriptive accounts and studies of CSA/incest survivors are based largely on samples of white young-to-middle-aged females. Other populations are severely underrepresented.

Male Victims

It is clear that male children also suffer from sexual abuse. Estimates based on general populations suggest that approximately 10-20% of males are sexually abused at some point in childhood (Finkelhor, 1979; Finkelhor, 1990). The average age of abuse has been estimated at 8-10 years (Finkelhor et al., 1989; Finkelhor, 1990; Hunter, 1991). However, the abuse of males tends to be underreported (Dimock, 1988; Finkelhor, 1984).

Research addressing the long-term effects of past abuse on adult males, although it is sparse, suggests that they may suffer consequences similar to those experienced by female survivors. Like females, male survivors may be somewhat overrepresented in psychiatric populations (Jacobson & Herald, 1990), and are described as being greatly affected in areas of sexual functioning (Dimock, 1988) and in marital disruption and nonreligiosity (Finkelhor et al., 1989). Several studies suggest that male survivors may be more likely than females to externalize anger or other emotional effects of abuse into aggressive behaviors (Briere, 1992a; Briere & Runtz, 1989; Zaidi, Knutson, & Mehm, 1989). In a clinical comparison study of males and females, Briere, Evans, Runtz, and Wall (1988) found no gender differences on general measures of dysfunction. Males, like females, experienced dissociation, anxiety, depression, sleep disturbances, and post-traumatic symptoms. Hunter's (1991) nonclinical comparison study paralleled these findings. Both male and female subjects exhibited more dysfunction on measures of self-esteem, sexual adjustment, and functioning in dyadic relationships than did nonabused controls. Males indicated higher levels of anxiety and worry and greater identity confusion than females.

Briere (1992a) notes that because of gender differences, males may differ from females in the ways that they cope with emotional effects and in their cognitive processing of the abusive experience(s). He suggests that interventions with male survivors should emphasize expression of sadness and fear, and provide assistance in dealing with the males' perceptions of having been stripped of their masculinity.

Geriatric Populations

Allers, Benjack, and Allers (1992) posit that residual abuse trauma may be underdetected in the elderly because it can easily be misdiagnosed as dementia or other psychopathologies. They suggest that, because many negative symptoms are viewed as "normal" in this population, caregivers and professionals may fail to recognize problems such as chronic depression, elder abuse, nightmares and sleep disturbances, and anxiety as possibly stemming from past abuse. These issues await empirical investigation.

Racial and Cultural Differences

Peters (1988) notes that research in this area seems to assume that Caucasian subjects' experience reflect the experiences of the majority of victims. Only a few studies have selected samples matching the specific ethnic composition of the given area (Wyatt, Guthrie, & Notgrass, 1992) or have addressed racial/cultural differences.

Russell, Schurman, and Trocki (1988), in a large, random, nonclinical sample, found that 16% of African-American and 17% of white women reported a history of childhood incest. The African-American women described the incest experience as more upsetting, and were more than three times as likely to have experienced severe abuse. They were also older at the time of abuse and there was more age disparity with their abusers. These factors may be associated with more severe subsequent symptomatology (Briere & Runtz, 1988a; Peters, 1988).

The Los Angeles Epidemiologic Catchment Area Study (Stein et al., 1988) revealed that, although Hispanic subjects reported overall lower rates of CSA than did non-Hispanic whites, a relatively higher proportion of Hispanic women had been victimized. The Hispanic victims, compared to whites, experienced increased occurrences of psychiatric diagnoses, substance abuse or dependency, affective disorders, anxiety, and phobia. These researchers speculate that, for the Hispanic victims, effects may have been exacerbated by low socioeconomic conditions and a greater reluctance to report abuse or seek treatment.

❏ Interpretation Issues and Research Suggestions

Most of the abuse effects research has been helpful to clinicians who attempt to understand and address the immediate concerns of clients who present with past-abuse issues (Alexander, 1992b). However, it is obvious that many research problems and issues remain. These problems and issues, which call for increased sophistication in terms of interpretation, conceptualization, and methodological rigor, clearly challenge our adherence to the "scientist-practitioner" model. In addition, we are challenged by a public that has begun to question the methods and assumptions of clinicians who work with abuse survivors.

REPRESENTATIVENESS OF SAMPLES

The use of either clinical or nonclinical samples results in various types of problems and issues. Results of studies using clinical samples may not be generalizable to a larger population. In addition, these samples may not include survivors of abuse who have not suffered deleterious effects. For example, in Herman et al.'s (1986) nonclinical outpatient sample, 50% of those who recalled CSA stated that they had recovered well, even though the abuse was upsetting. None of them would likely have been included in a clinical sample. Community samples enhance generalizability, but may represent a population distinct from those who seek treatment. Although community samples do suggest patterns of functioning and relationships, they may give little insight into the underlying dimensions of abuse (Cole & Putnam, 1992).

Obviously, both clinical and nonclinical studies may need to rely on retrospective information concerning details of the abuse and family functioning. For example, subjects in Murphy et al.'s (1988) study reported that the onset of their abuse occurred an average of 37 years prior to the study. Retrospective accounts, however, may be inaccurate and subject to memory loss or denial (Alexander, 1992a; Beutler & Hill, 1992; Briere, 1992b). Samples of survivors who present to treatment programs may not include victims who are in extreme denial or who have amnesia regarding their abuse (Briere, 1992b; Draucker, 1989).

Generalizability may also be limited by inconsistencies in defining abuse and by variations in age groups used in samples (Briere, 1992b). For example, Briere and Runtz (1988b) include, in their sample, persons who recall abuse up to age 15; Saunders et al. (1992) include persons victimized up to the age of 18.

INDIVIDUAL CHARACTERISTICS OF VICTIMS

Age and Developmental Factors

Cole and Putman (1992) posit that apparent inconsistencies found in the effects literature may reflect a failure to consider developmental factors. They argue that various disorders reflect impairments in self-concept and social development that may vary by developmental status, and that these likely cannot be ferreted out by symptom checklists. They suggest that abuse needs to be considered in terms of the developmental transitions across which it occurred.

Studies that examine differences based on age alone have thus far yielded conflicting results. Several studies suggest that abuse at an older age is associated with greater problems in adulthood (Murphy et al., 1988; Peters, 1988; Wyatt & Newcomb, 1990). However, it has also been suggested that abuse at a younger age may contribute to amnesia and may result in delayed treatment (Kendall-Tackett, 1991).

Individual cognitive abilities are related to developmental status. Cognitive abilities are stressed as possible "protective factors" (Garmezy, 1983) and are seen as being capable of affecting a child's ability to perceive accurately and cope with stressors (Horowitz, 1976). Cognitive factors that contribute to susceptibility may also increase the likelihood of damage (Finkelhor, 1984). Therefore, it may be important to look at individual cognitive evaluations of abuse and their relationship to later adjustment. Harter et al. (1988) found that increased perceptions of social isolation predicted later social maladjustments. Draucker (1989) determined that, for female incest survivors, mastery of certain cognitive tasks at the time of abuse was related to adult functioning.

Attachment

Alexander (1992b) suggests that attachment theory might provide a helpful basis for understanding the differential consequences of abuse as they relate to attachments at various stages of development. Alexander cautions that attachment theory will assume some causality between childhood and adult experiences and will be subject to sampling and measurement problems inherent in this type of research in general.

Type and Severity of the Abuse

A number of studies suggest that abuse that is more severe (usually defined in terms of force or invasiveness) or is longer lasting will have more deleterious and prolonged consequences (Finkelhor, Hotaling, Lewis, & Smith, 1990; Herman et al., 1986; Peters, 1988; Saunders et al., 1992). Terr (1991) distinguishes between Type I childhood traumas, or "single blows," which involve detailed memories, omens, and perceptions and Type II childhood traumas, which result from repeated exposures and lead to symptoms such as denial, numbing, dissociation, and rage. Terr states that, left untreated, all but the very mildest traumas have the capacity to produce long-lasting patterns of misperceptions, fears, and cognitive patterns that may result in pathology.

Wyatt and Newcomb (1990) addressed the complex interactions of various circumstances of sexual abuse (age, severity, duration, proximity, coercion, and teenaged perpetrator) and mediator variables (immediate negative responses, internal attributions, disclosure of the abuse, and involvement of authorities). They found that both severity of abuse and proximity to the perpetrator were related to adult functioning. Involvement of authorities did not function as a mediator. Briere and Runtz (1990) found that physical, sexual, and emotional abuse resulted in different types of effects, each in its own way damaging. Unfortunately, studies often fail to differentiate between types of abuse, and often lack accurate or consistent definitions.

FACTORS RELATED TO THE ABUSIVE SITUATIONS

Relationship to Perpetrator

It is assumed that initially being in a close and trusting relationship to the perpetrator may render abuse more harmful because of an increased sense of betrayal. In addition, the ready accessibility of the victim to the perpetrator may lead to repeated offenses (Coker, 1990; Cole & Putnam, 1992; Finkelhor, 1979). A number of studies suggest that proximity (or being related) is a significant factor that contributes to the impact of the abuse. Cole and Putnam (1992) found father-daughter abuse to be longer-lasting and more deleterious than nonfamilial abuse. In a nonclinical outpatient sample, Herman et al. (1986) found abuse by a paternal figure was related to long-term negative effects. Wyatt and Newcomb (1990) obtained similar results with a clinical sample. In a controlled study with a nonclinical sample, Harter et al. (1988) accounted for significant family and social-cognitive factors and still found that paternal incest was linked to poor social adjustment.

Bushnell et al. (1992) found familial abuse to be related to depression, substance abuse, and disordered eating. Briere and Runtz (1988a) determined that parental abuse was linked to anxiety. Parker and Parker (1991) found that, on measures of social adjustment, maladjustment increased progressively among nonabused subjects, nonfamilial abuse victims, and incest victims. Likewise, Lundberg-Love et al. (1992) found higher levels of pathology in subjects who were incestuously abused than in those who were nonincestuously abused. Despite these apparent differences in consequences, many studies fail to distinguish between familial and nonfamilial abuse.

Family Functioning

Alexander (1985) notes that many variables in incestuous families, independent of the abuse, result in problems. In general, families in which abuse occurs have been found to be dysfunctional. Harter et al. (1988) found these families to be lacking in both cohesion and adaptability. Madonna, Van Scoyk, and Jones (1991) note that incest families are more dysfunctional than nonincest families on a range of measures, including those addressing belief systems, level of emotional support, and conflict resolution.

Family Psychopathology

Related to the issue of family functioning variables is the concern that the high levels of pathology assessed in survivors of abuse may be strongly influenced either by genetic predisposition to psychopathology or by environmental factors that result from its presence in the home environment. Sexual abuse tends to occur in families with a history of psychiatric problems (Brown & Anderson, 1991; Kinzl & Biebl, 1991). However, it is not clear whether later pathology is exclusively the result of these tendencies, or whether it is alone sufficient cause for problems to develop. In an attempt to address this question, Scott and Stone (1986) found, in incest families, that the abused daughters' Minnesota Multiphasic Personality Inventory (MMPI) profiles were more elevated and differed most significantly from other family members' profiles.

RESEARCH SUGGESTIONS

Design

Most current research relies on cross-sectional designs, correlations, and/or retrospective data. Whenever possible, longitudinal designs should be utilized (Briere, 1992b; Cole & Putman, 1992; Finkelhor, 1990). Both short-term and long-term prospective studies involving observations of identified cases are needed (Cole & Putnam, 1992). Either equivalent control groups should be used, or comparison groups (e.g., abused versus nonabused) should be drawn from the same population (Briere, 1992b; Pribor & Dinwiddie, 1992).

Samples

Within samples, definitions of abuse should be exact and consistent, and factors related to type of abuse, proximity, duration, and indications of severity should be assessed. Risk factors possibly related to effects such as family functioning, age, or developmental status, individual coping skills, revictimizations, and other concurrent abuse should also be assessed (Alexander, 1992a; Cole & Putnam, 1992; Parker & Parker, 1991). To enhance generalizability, more research needs to focus on populations that receive less attention, including males, older adults, and persons of various racial and socioeconomic groups (Finkelhor, 1990; Wyatt et al., 1992).

Measures

Instruments used to measure symptomatology should be valid, reliable, standardized, and specific to abuse-relevant issues. In many cases, reliance on retrospective reports is unavoidable. When this is the case, it may be helpful to attempt to account for the effects of amnesia, denial, memory loss, age-related socialization, or any obvious motivations to fabricate accounts (Briere, 1992b).

Statistics

Briere (1992b) contends that differences between abused and nonabused subjects may be underestimated in smaller samples. In general, samples used in assessing effects and incidence or prevalence data need to be larger (Finkelhor et al., 1990). Studies in this area will generally benefit from attempts to increase statistical power, from the use of multivariate analyses to ferret out complex relationships in larger samples, and from the careful use of statistical controls for partialing out variables (e.g., family factors) to avoid erroneous assumptions of causality (Briere, 1988, 1992b).

❏ Overview of Incest Therapy Groups

Reports indicate that incest therapy groups have taken a variety of forms and theoretical bases, have utilized various formats, and have differed in terms of duration, composition, and assessment of outcome. The following sections review the available research literature on group therapy with this population. The types of groups that have been utilized are described, the results of existing treatment outcome studies are reviewed, and some relevant issues and controversies are discussed.

RATIONALE FOR GROUP TREATMENT

Courtois (1988) recommends group treatment for incest survivors because this experience alleviates secrecy, isolation, and stigmatization, and thereby facilitates resolution of the trauma. According to Briere (1989), as group members help one another, self-esteem is enhanced and members begin to feel less deviant. The opportunity to receive feedback from peers, to build meaningful relationships, and to share common experiences is also of benefit to this population (Courtois & Leehan, 1982; Drews & Bradley, 1989; Fowler, Burns, &

Roehl, 1983). Group therapy may also provide a means for regaining a sense of personal power and reducing feelings of helplessness (Kriedler & England, 1990) and may provide an ideal environment for working through relationship issues (Deighton & McPeek, 1985; Hays, 1987). Involvement in group may also facilitate the working through of new memories (Briere, 1988; Courtois, 1992).

Two studies note that Yalom's (1985) therapeutic factors may be applicable to these groups. Bonney, Randall, and Cleveland (1986) found that self-understanding, cohesiveness, corrective recapitulation of the primary family group, catharsis, universality, and existential factors were all relevant to their therapy group. Likewise, Wheeler, O'Malley, Waldo, Murphy, and Blank (1992) determined that catharsis, self-understanding, the existential factor, and cohesiveness were perceived as important by group members and were also related to various group stages.

DESCRIPTIVE ACCOUNTS

At present, over 80% of available sources that discuss incest therapy groups present descriptive accounts of these groups. These articles tend to provide anecdotal evaluations, postgroup satisfaction questionnaires, or no evaluation at all. However, this literature, which includes the earliest accounts of these groups, offers much practical and theoretical guidance in what is still a relatively new area of practice.

MODELS AND PROGRAMS

A number of descriptive reports present specific models for group treatment. Goodman and Nowak-Scibelli (1985) introduced a time-limited structural model. The goal of these groups was to decrease shame and guilt, facilitate identification, enhance coping skills, improve relationships, and prevent further incest. No results were presented.

McBride and Emerson (1989) describe a 3-stage model for long-term group therapy that focused on trust development, emotional release, and cognitive restructuring. Clients in their program reported improvements in positive feelings, sexual functioning, intimacy, and assertiveness. A model for a short-term group that focuses on amelioration of PTSD symptoms is described by Cole and Barney (1987). Kriedler and England (1990) and Kriedler and Hassan (1992) developed a long-term (56-session) program. Their model, which emphasizes empowerment and behavior change, was reported to increase the clients' sense of self-esteem and empowerment.

Coker (1990); Giaretto (1981); Fowler et al. (1983); and Hall, Kassees, and Hoffman (1986) also describe incest survivor groups as part of larger treatment programs. Several comprehensive programs include adjunct groups for significant others of survivors (including partners) (Brittain & Merriam, 1988; Cohen, 1988) and joint family therapy (Coker, 1990).

Short-Term Groups

One of the earliest short-term incest treatment groups is described by Tsai and Wagner (1978), who offered a series of 4-session groups to 50 adult survivors. Their 6-month follow-up questionnaire indicated that clients experienced improved relationships and decreased guilt. Other short-term groups are described by Herman and Schatzow (1984), Gordy (1983), and Knight (1990). Participants felt Knight's group diminished isolation, and improved self-esteem, belonging, optimism, and intimacy.

Descriptions indicate that short-term incest treatment groups tend to be structured and goal oriented. Cole (1985) overviews a 6-week structured support group that participants reported was helpful in building self-esteem, trust, and assertion. Drews and Bradley (1989) utilized a structured, educational format in which goal setting was emphasized. Axelroth's (1991) 8-week structured group for college students addressed commonalities, after effects, and emotional issues. Brandt (1989) used a semistructured, theme-focused format found by participants to be highly effective.

Long-Term Groups

We consider groups that meet more than 12 weeks long-term groups. Descriptive accounts of these groups indicate that most are somewhat unstructured. Swink and Leveille (1986) overview a

7-step rebuilding process that takes place in their 18-week group format. They place an emphasis on bonding, power, and cultural issues. Open-ended process groups include those of Abney, Yang, and Paulson (1992), which explored roles and images and involved family enactments; Hays (1987), which combined psychodynamic and cognitive-behavioral techniques; and Bergart (1986), which focused on themes including fear, self-blame, power,and intimacy, and was reported to produce reductions in shame, guilt, and isolation. Long-term groups (Blake-White & Kline, 1985; Laube & Wieland, 1990) were also conducted for CSA survivors diagnosed with bulimia.

UNCONTROLLED CLINICAL
OUTCOME STUDIES

Outcome studies that provide some empirical data, primarily in the form of pre- and post-treatment questionnaires, have typically assessed the benefits of time-limited therapy groups. Douglas and Matson (1989) evaluated a 10-week process group led by a male-female cotherapist team. Results, which were limited by the small sample and incomplete pretreatment questionnaires, failed to find significant differences in measures of general distress. However, participants indicated that they felt the group provided support and reduced isolation and guilt.

Roberts and Lie (1989) also conducted 10-session groups that were largely unstructured, but had general therapeutic goals such as "promoting trust" or "reclaiming the child." Significant differences were found in self-assessment measures of psychosocial, physical, and sexual functioning in postgroup tests. Depression scales decreased significantly for most participants (but increased for more than 28%). Improvements noted at postgroup tests were stable at 6 months. Apolinsky and Wilcoxon's (1991) Intervention Program also was assessed in terms of outcome on measures of depression and general functioning. They compared the results of two structured 10-week eclectic group therapy formats with and without symbolic confrontation activities with the offending parent. Pre- and post-treatment analyses suggest that the symbolic confrontation component was effective in ameliorating negative symptoms, including depression and negative self-evaluations. No treatment effect was found for eclectic therapy alone.

One exception to the typical 10-week formats described above is that of Carver, Stalker, Stewart, and Abraham (1989). They began their program with a 10-week format but later expanded it to 15 weeks. Groups were led by several different leaders and varied in terms of composition, structure, and content. Focus was on the disclosure of painful memories and feelings, and the discussion of common themes including trust, sexuality, self-esteem, and anger. Participation in group was found to result in significant post-test differences on a number of variables including somatization, depression, anxiety, hostility, psychoticism, and global symptomatology.

The outcome of the Village's treatment program as presented in this book has also been evaluated (Donaldson & Edwards, 1988). One-hundred and seventy-nine clients were assessed at intake using the Beck Depression Inventory (BDI, Beck, 1978), the State-Trait Anxiety Inventory (STAI, Spielberger, Gorsuch, Lushene, Vagg, & Jacobs, 1968), and the Response to Childhood Incest Questionnaire (RCIQ, Edwards & Donaldson, 1989). The clients were reassessed at various intervals throughout treatment and at post-treatment. Results suggest that the levels of symptoms varied throughout the course of treatment, showing a characteristic pattern. Measures on the RCIQ (which assesses general functioning and PTSD symptoms) showed an increase in the number and severity of symptoms early in treatment; however, symptoms ameliorated and then stabilized after an average of 6 to 7 months of treatment.

CONTROLLED CLINICAL OUTCOME STUDIES

At present, we are aware of only one group treatment program that has systematically assessed outcomes using a control group. In a program that involved 65 clients and eight pairs of group leaders, a 10-week process group format was compared with a more structured interpersonal transaction group format and a wait-list control group (Alexander, Neimeyer, Follette, Moore, & Harter, 1989; Alexander, Neimeyer, & Follette, 1991; Follette, Alexander, & Follette, 1991). Results on four standardized scales suggest that both treatment conditions were more effective than the wait-list condition in reducing depression and general distress and in enhancing social adjustment. Gains were maintained at 6 months. These authors speculate that a structured format may be beneficial for novice clients who may be highly anxious. Process group may be best suited to clients who have already made gains in therapy. These authors suggest that a less-structured format, under the guidance of a skilled leader, may increase generalizability of positive outcomes. They also note that clients who benefited most were single, more educated, had had previous treatment, suffered less severe abuse, or were initially better adjusted.

❑ General Issues

THEORETICAL BASES

Examples of group approaches for incest survivors include Ericksonian therapy and hypnosis (Gilligan & Kennedy, 1989), experiential approaches (Kearney-Cooke, 1988), educational formats (Fowler et al., 1983), psychodynamic techniques (Bonney et al., 1986), cognitive-behavioral formats (Drews & Bradley, 1989; Jehu, 1988), and process groups (Alexander, Neimeyer, Follette, Moore, & Harter, 1989; Alexander, Neimeyer, & Follette, 1991). With the exception of the work of Alexander, Neimeyer, Follette, Moore, and Harter (1989) and Alexander, Neimeyer, and Follette (1991), the relative merits of various approaches have not been empirically evaluated.

THERAPISTS

Most groups for female incest survivors have been led by female therapists. Cole (1985) recommends the use of a female therapist because a male might unintentionally revictimize clients. Coker (1990) argues that a female therapist is the best role model for this population. Similarly, Brandt (1989) asserts that the presence of a female therapist enhances trust, safety, and positive gender identity. Conversely, Hunter (1991) suggests using only male therapist for an all-male treatment group.

Laube and Wieland (1990) contend that a treatment team may provide positive modeling of good relationships, tolerance, objectivity, and healthy boundaries. Douglas and Matson (1989) and Deighton and McPeek (1985) advocate the use of a male/female cotherapist team. Courtois (1988) contradicts this, mentioning that the presence of even one male cotherapist may inhibit trust and cohesiveness in the group. Although suggestions regarding therapist gender or use of cotherapists may be helpful, the relative usefulness of male therapists or cotherapists has not been empirically investigated.

COMPOSITION OF GROUPS

Most groups discussed in the current literature consist of adult female survivors. Exceptions include all-male groups (Hunter, 1991; Singer, 1989) and groups composed of both males and females (Apolinsky & Wilcoxon, 1991; Gilligan & Kennedy, 1989; Goodman & Nowak-Scibelli, 1985).

Groups generally consist of 4 to 9 members, with 6 to 8 being the standard. Interestingly, with the exception of Hunter's (1991) group, groups that include male members have been slightly larger. Singer's (1989) male group consisted of 13 members; mixed-gender groups (Apolinsky & Wilcoxon, 1991; Gilligan & Kennedy, 1989; Goodman & Nowack-Scibelli, 1985) have accepted up to 10 members.

It is believed that limiting group membership fosters cohesiveness (Yalom, 1985) and allows sufficient time for individual needs to be met (Corey, 1985). Briere (1989) cautions against inclusion of more than 10 or fewer than 4 members. However, this issue has not been systematically explored.

DURATION OF GROUPS

As a general rule, groups that have been in any way systematically assessed are those of shorter duration. In addition, most of the early groups for this population have been short-term groups that have focused primarily on providing information, dispelling secrecy, alleviating shame and guilt, and decreasing isolation and stigma. The formation of many of these groups was likely prompted by a growing awareness of the seriousness of the problem of past abuse as well as by the need to validate and address its effects. The short-term approach has many advocates. For example, Herman and Schatzow (1984) argue that a short-term format provides pressure that expedites bonding. They add that a shorter duration of treatment limits the amount of time during which the lives of participants will be in upheaval. Cole (1985) suggests that, although a longer-term group may better allow processing of issues, short-term groups enhance trust by not allowing conflicts to develop. However, clients in Cole's program indicated the need for further therapy.

Other therapists insist that, although short-term groups have their merits, true growth and lasting change may require more time and experience. According to Hall et al. (1986), long-term groups allow for continued growth. Newer members benefit from the experience and modeling of old members. Ganzarain and Buchele (1987) and Abney et al. (1992) argue that a long-term process is necessary for both acting out and transference issues to be addressed. Axelroth (1991) notes that for some clients, a short tenure in group may serve to exacerbate symptoms. Longer experiences may allow these clients more time to process issues and gain coping skills.

In their research, Alexander et al. (1989, 1991) and Follette et al. (1991) note that for many clients, gains made in short-term treatment were not sufficient to preclude the need for continued therapy. They suggest that, to allow group members to work through family issues, experience new forms of interaction, gain support and insight, develop trust, grieve losses, overcome shame and stigma, alter negative patterns of beliefs, and make lasting behavioral changes, considerable time must be spent involved in the group process.

> *Both resources and goals influence decisions about the duration of a group.*

The decision to offer a long-term group, as opposed to a shorter one, may depend on available resources as well as on the ultimate goals of the group experience. If the primary function of the group is to provide relief from the traumatic effects of abuse, to reduce isolation and self-blame, and to dispel basic misconceptions, a short-term group may be advised. A short-term group may also be appropriate for clients who already possess good ego strength, insight, and an adequate support system. However, if time and resources are available, a long-term group may facilitate the recovery process by providing a corrective developmental experience as well as an excellent environment for learning and change.

INDIVIDUAL THERAPY

As a general rule, individual therapy is highly recommended in conjunction with group therapy (Abney et al., 1992; Coker, 1990; Courtois, 1988; Goodman & Nowack-Scibelli, 1985). Obviously, many issues can be addressed in more depth on an individual basis than in group. Some clients will also need to learn to trust an individual therapist before they can begin to trust people in a group (Courtois, 1988). Others may need progress with some individual issues or to move out of crisis before they are ready for group. Specific issues regarding the relative effectiveness of individual versus group therapy, the timing and duration of individual treatment, and the interface of the two modalities remain to be studied.

❑ Summary

As Cahill, Llewelyn, and Pearson (1991) report, the literature on group therapy for incest survivors is rich with ideas and techniques relevant to addressing the issues of this population. Therapists generally agree on goals and therapeutic issues. However, there is a dearth of systematic data obtained from controlled studies.

Clearly, this lack of empirical rigor reflects the current developmental stage of work in this treatment modality. Once the need for therapy for this population was identified, attempts were made to address its unique issues and symptoms within the limits of available resources. As a consequence, too many programs have relied on client-satisfaction questionnaires rather than on standardized assessments as primary outcome measures. Others have not standardized treatment protocols within or across groups or have failed to use equivalent control groups.

According to Beutler and Hill (1992), outcome research must comply with commonly accepted state-of-the-art principles, including:

1. use of representative samples,
2. use of valid and reliable instruments for measurement,
3. avoidance of the use of designs that result in low statistical power or redundant data,
4. standardization of descriptions and applications of treatments,
5. larger therapist samples, and
6. protection against researcher biases.

Process research should examine the effects of therapist behaviors, client variables and behaviors, and the nature of the therapeutic relationship. Valid and reliable assessment instruments and objective ratings of events and processes must also be used.

Treatment programs need to begin to address specific research avenues systematically, including relative merits of various group formats, length of treatment, impact of type and severity of abuse, severity of symptoms and age on group treatment outcomes, groups for specific subpopulations, effects of individual characteristics or abilities of group members on outcome, and relative merits of the various components of comprehensive treatment packages. As an attempt to contribute to this process and to assist other group therapists in working with groups in testable formats, we present our incest treatment program and our working models for organizing and conducting group therapy.

2

Getting Started

Our experience in working with therapy groups suggests that the ultimate success of such a group depends largely on all that precedes it. *In our program, three stages of early therapy and preparation take place prior to the first therapy group session: the conceptual stage, the formation stage, and the pretherapy group.*

❑ Conceptual Stage

During the conceptual stage, the therapist professionally and personally prepares to lead the group. Clients begin individual therapy sessions, assessments, and education.

THERAPIST PREPARATION

A number of issues regarding the therapist's personal background, professional knowledge and skills, and the work environment should

33

be addressed prior to forming a group. The therapist needs to understand what professional and personal aspects she or he brings into the group and how her or his skills may best be used in this modality. The therapist also needs to be aware of and plan for the particular challenges this type of group may present.

Professional Background

Any mental health professional who plans to conduct a therapy group for survivors of incest should be well versed in various theoretical orientations as well as in individual, group, and family therapy techniques. Formal course work in human development, psychopathology, systems theory, group dynamics, victimization, and women's issues is also particularly helpful in working with this population. The therapist should have in-depth knowledge regarding the etiology and treatment of the long-term effects of child sexual abuse. Leaders of incest groups may benefit from previous experience with other types of groups.

Professionals who work with this population come from a variety of backgrounds and may differ in the types of approaches they use. Although a number of approaches are applicable to this population (see chapter 1), the overall attitude and abilities of the therapist may be as important as the specific approach used.

Personal Issues

Many professional programs, for practical or philosophical reasons, do not focus on therapists' personal issues as part of their formal education. Therapists beginning to work with incest survivors need to consider how they personally will be affected by the content of the abuse or the intensity of the recovery process. Working within a supportive milieu is essential. Support for the therapist may include individual therapy, a treatment team, or personal supervision.

From its inception, our program has consistently involved the use of a staff support system. The therapists who conduct the groups meet formally on a weekly basis (usually for about 1 ½ hours). These meetings not only provide a venue for reviewing the progress of the groups and receiving insights and suggestions regarding individual and group issues, but they also have become a forum for expressing individual frustrations, emotional reactions, and concerns.

Listening repeatedly to accounts of atrocities and neglect experienced by our clients is difficult, especially when we think of our own lives and loved ones. The support system allows us to vent our emotional reactions and to maintain equilibrium. This, in turn, allows us to balance objectivity with empathy and to maintain appropriate boundaries when we work with our clients.

We will never cease to feel anger and grief on behalf of our clients and should probably not work with abuse if we become so cold and hardened that we do not respond to the feelings of victims. However, we find that, with practice, the therapists in our program develop good personal coping skills that allow them to handle the emotional fallout as they work with this population. Having sufficient support allows one to process necessary information and to "leave it at the office," and, most importantly, to exercise appropriate boundaries.

Survivors versus nonsurvivors as therapists. Clients and professionals alike raise the issue of whether a therapist in an incest treatment program should or should not be a survivor. Some believe that it is necessary to have experienced this type of trauma in order to truly understand the process that a victim experiences. Others argue that a survivor, even after considerable treatment, may be too close to the issues to be a truly objective helper (Briere, 1989). Certainly, either situation can be an asset or a liability. Being a nonsurvivor might be a liability if one cannot identify with a victim's feelings; however, this does not mean that the nonsurvivor therapist cannot be well informed, sensitive, and empathic. To argue that only a victim should treat another is akin to arguing that one must be depressed to treat depression. A person who has experienced depression may naturally have empathy, but will not necessarily be a more competent therapist because of that experience. A therapist (survivor or not) is likely to be effective if she or he is aware of the issues facing survivors, has empathy, is able to set appropriate boundaries, is sufficiently skilled, and understands gender and power issues. When this is the case, clients who initially express concerns regarding the therapist's history may be reassured (Courtois, 1988).

Therapists who are survivors of incest or any other earlier trauma should be careful to do their own work well before attempting to work with this population. A past victim will naturally identify strongly with clients. To be an effective therapist, she or he must be able to set clear personal boundaries and be free from any symptoms that would interfere with the ability to function fully as a professional. Support is of utmost importance for the survivor therapist. It may be helpful for the support or supervisory system to include a nonsurvivor who can objectively point out when issues become too close.

Gender. More often than not, female survivors state that they feel more comfortable and safe with a female therapist (Cahill et al., 1991). A female therapist may also affirm the process of women helping and empowering one another. It is, however, possible for female therapists to overidentify with female clients (Briere, 1989). Male survivors may also seek out a female therapist because they may feel that revealing their victimization to a male will be extremely humiliating (Kaplan, Becker, & Tenke, 1991). On the other hand, working with a male therapist can help a client work through issues such as power, safety, and sexuality. The male therapist should understand and encourage the client's need to be empowered, to express anger toward males, and to form a truly safe relationship with the male (Briere, 1989; Courtois & Watts, 1982).

Obviously, as is the case with the therapist-survivor, the therapist's gender can be either an asset or a liability. Our experience suggests that a male therapist can make an excellent coleader for an all-female group in the latter stages of the therapy process. At that point, most group members will likely be more confident and ready to address gender issues more directly.

Working context. Other factors that merit consideration in preparing to conduct a therapy group are related to the context in which the group is to be conducted. Arrangements that may be helpful for the therapist include:

- Compensatory time or scheduled downtime to alleviate stress and to allow processing

- A network of others who also work with victims
- A personal support group or therapist
- A schedule that includes a percentage of clients or groups whose problems require less emotionally intensive work
- Increased vacation time or shorter work hours

We also insist that our clients who have multiple diagnoses (e.g., those who are chemically dependent) be involved in an outside support system. At times, working with survivors will require extensive collateral time, particularly for multiple-problem clients. Staffing, supervision, and other self-care time should be considered part of the total treatment time both emotionally and economically. Overall, the therapist needs to be assured that the agency will provide sufficient time, space, and funding for the program.

Conceptual Issues

Leading therapy groups can be a demanding task. Each group is a unique system in which members interact to meet their own needs and to help each other. In attempting to attend to each member's needs while nurturing the group as a whole, the therapist may feel overwhelmed by the intense and often conflicting needs presented. To remain clearly in a leader's role and to make the most beneficial therapeutic choices regarding content and process issues, the therapist needs to maintain a sense of direction. To assist in this, we have formulated two organizational frameworks. One framework, the **4 Ms for therapists**, delineates the functions of the group leader. The other framework, the **PGI model**, categorizes common content issues presented during incest therapy groups.

The 4 Ms for therapists. We find the 4 Ms to be a simple and easy-to-remember way to explain the role of the therapist in groups.

The 4 Ms (messenger, monitor, mediator, and member) describe functions that the therapist performs as a part of facilitating the group process. We separate these functions primarily for the ease of explanation. In reality, they are simultaneous and interdependent components of the therapist's entire behavioral repertoire as well as

Table 2.1   The 4Ms for Group Therapists

The Messenger Function: The therapist is a messenger via:
  A. Modeling: Demonstrating helping skills, empathy, boundaries
  B. Teaching: Describing pertinent research and theory, the recovery process, cultural issues

The Monitor Function: The therapist monitors the group process by:
  A. Observing: Maintaining vigilance over all functions of the group and its members
  B. Analyzing: Analyzing what has been observed in terms of basic belief themes of *power, goodness,* and *importance*

The Mediator Function: The therapist mediates group process by:
  A. Acting: Engaging in appropriate behaviors based on analysis of observations
  B. Activating: Facilitating client helping behaviors, actions, problem solving

The Member Function: The therapist is a distinct member of the group who functions as such by:
  A. Participating: Being an active part of the system with clear professional boundaries
  B. Learning: Developing professional and personal knowledge as a result of participating in the group process

---

part of her or his inner thought processes. The four functions are summarized in Table 2.1 and described in depth below.

The messenger function. The therapist functions as a messenger by modeling behaviors and teaching concepts. Therefore, the functions of the messenger are both direct and indirect, verbal and nonverbal, and perhaps intentional as well as unintentional. One can assume that the more anxious and unsure a group member is, the more likely she will be to watch and listen to the leader for clues about what to do, how to react, and how to behave acceptably.

Modeling. As a helping professional, the therapist is a natural model of behaviors that will allow clients to help one another and to use group appropriately. Through the therapist's example, the group members may observe basic listening skills, empathic and respectful responding, problem solving, appropriate emotional expression, and acknowledgment of the worth of each group member. Group also offers the opportunity for members to observe ways in which the leader maintains healthy boundaries when helping others. In addition, when the leader accepts the leadership role but does not abuse power, members observe that power does not have to be abusive.

Teaching. As a professional with expertise regarding the issues relevant to an incest survivors' group, the therapist is a natural teacher. She or he can be a resource person on information regarding relevant theory and research on group process, the recovery process, pertinent sys-temic and cultural issues, and the like. Clients typically ask a number of questions of the group leader. However, as is discussed later, it is important not to jump too readily into the role of "the authority." At times, members will learn more about themselves and the group process when they are asked, "Why are you asking that question at this time?" Discussion of a process question may produce more interaction than jumping in with facts and figures. It is also helpful to separate teaching time from the group process itself.

The monitor function. The second important function of the group therapist is to serve as a monitor. This is primarily an internal process that involves observation and analysis of the content, process, emotional level, and interactions of the group and its subsystems. If this sounds like a tall order, it is. Obviously no one person, no matter how well trained or experienced, can have eyes, ears, and thoughts everywhere at once. Although a cotherapist may be helpful in assisting with the monitoring process, the therapist and group members alike need to understand that no therapist can be omniscient. Only so much can be seen, understood, and dealt with at one time. Important issues that somehow get passed over seem to have a tendency to re-emerge and can be dealt with in due time. An organizational model such as the PGI framework, discussed below, may also be of help with the monitoring function.

Observing. As an observer, the therapist maintains vigilance in regard to the overall functioning of the group. This vigilance involves observation of process and content alike. The therapist notes patterns of consistency and inconsistency by observing which members tend to dominate conversations, what topics are typically introduced, and how members react to certain topics. The therapist also notes the sequence of interactions (e.g., who speaks first). In addition, the therapist observes the rules, roles, and other structural aspects of the group such as subgrouping and deviant members. Questions the therapist should continually consider while observing include:

1. Who speaks?
2. When do they speak?
3. Who responds?
4. Who is silent?
5. What nonverbal language do I see?
6. What is the tone or emotional climate of the conversation?
7. What subjects are being introduced? When? By whom?
8. What are possible hidden agendas?
9. Who is being addressed?
10. Who is being looked at? By whom?
11. Are all members engaged in the process?
12. Is feedback positive or negative?

These types of observational questions address what is taking place at all levels, including the group as a whole, subsystems of the group (dyads, triads), and the individual group member.

Analyzing. As the functioning of the group is being observed, the therapist forms flexible hypotheses regarding the meaning of the content as well as the interactions or processes. Primary questions involve "why" and may include:

1. Why is this particular subject being discussed now?
2. Why don't verbalizations match behavior?
3. Why is the member silent?
4. What else might she mean?
5. Why is the group behaving this way?

Hypotheses reflect the therapist's answers to these questions. Sometimes the answer may involve the group as a whole; other times it may focus on individual members or subgroups.

Because group interactions are complex, the therapist juggles multiple hypotheses simultaneously. Choosing which hypothesis to explore is part of the analysis function. For example, in one group the therapist observes that members are particularly silent during the group. One member looks very sad while other members look lost and distant. When members speak, they seem to be talking about issues involving safety. The therapist hypothesizes that the member looking sad may be reacting to a recent abusive incident with her husband. The therapist further hypothesizes that the group may be silent because the emotional intensity of topics seems overwhelming. At this point, the therapist must choose which hypothesis to explore first. In making this choice, she or he must consider the needs of the sad member and the needs of the group as a whole. No hard and fast rules about choosing the "correct" hypotheses exist. We advise, however, that the therapist have some observable evidence to support the hypothesis and that an exploration of hypotheses be tentative, reflect the therapist's curiosity, and display willingness to consider alternative explanations.

The mediator function. Once the therapist has observed, processed, and analyzed, she or he, as mediator, acts either by responding in appropriate ways or by activating responses in the group.

Acting. The group therapist acts on the information observed and analyzed by engaging in behaviors appropriate to the situation. Such actions may include testing hypotheses, requesting clarification, providing feedback, posing related questions, and presenting relevant information. Acting involves the therapist's externalization of the processes that were internalized as monitor. In the above example, the therapist chose to focus on the group as a whole by saying, "The group is particularly silent tonight and most of you seem far away. Does the silence mean that you are feeling overwhelmed by something?" Or the therapist may choose not to state the hypothesis but may simply ask for further clarification by saying, "I'm wondering what the silence means?"

Activating. The therapist activates therapeutic client interactions by promoting helping behaviors among members; by facilitating resolution of conflict, miscommunication, and problem solving; and by challenging the group members to respond via communication or action. Strategic interventions may be used to activate changes within the group and are most effective if the intervention moves the focus to "here and now" interactions (Yalom, 1985). In the above example, the therapist may choose to activate the group by saying, "Kate has been looking very sad. How can you help Kate with sadness? Kate, how can the group help you?" With these activating comments, the members are brought to a here-and-now focus and reminded of their responsibility to be helpful group members.

The member function. The therapist is a member in two primary ways. As a group leader, the therapist is a participant and learner in the group process, but is in a role distinct from that of other members. The therapist is also a member as she or he participates in a treatment team or support staff. The group leader keeps the team informed of the progress and concerns regarding the group. Learning experiences are also shared with the treatment team.

Participating. The therapist is clearly in a professional role and exercises appropriate limits regarding disclosure of personal issues. However, she or he is still a participant in the group. To be perceived as sincerely interested in members' recovery, the leader must display genuine emotional reactions to the content and process of the group. These genuine reactions to and interactions with the group are a necessary and integral part of the group process. When therapists accept the member function and are emotionally available to members, they can help to intensify members' emotional involvement in the group. Again, continuing with the earlier example, the therapist mediated only after feeling the sadness and emotional distance in the room. In line with the member function, the therapist may intervene by saying, "I'm sensing both sadness and a feeling of emotional distance in the group. Are any of you?" Such mediations not only assist the group to deeper involvement in the process, but they demonstrate to the group the therapist's involvement in the ongoing process. The therapist will need to continue to rely on membership in a support system to deal with personal emotional issues brought up by working with the group.

Learning. Through involvement with the group process, the therapist continues to develop professional knowledge and skills. Because no two groups are alike, each becomes a fertile ground for learning and growth. Such growth also often takes place on a personal (but private) level. As issues are dealt with in group, the therapist gains understanding and insight regarding her or his own similar issues. Participation in the treatment team or a support network also enhances the learning process via staffing of particular sessions or clients and through sharing of insights and information.

In summary, the therapist can use the 4 Ms as a guide in deciding what type of behavioral response is most therapeutic. Because all functions occur simultaneously, the therapist should continually survey each function. Because the therapist deals at all times with a complex and dynamic system, the simple-to-remember mnemonic should be helpful in observing and analyzing complex issues. How these functions are played out is explained in greater detail in chapter 4.

The Power, Goodness, and Importance (PGI) Model. We have also devised a framework that guides therapists in understanding and directing the content of group discussions. In working with our groups, we found that, although we wanted to give members maximum freedom to present topics important to them, we often felt overwhelmed by the divergence of topics presented. For example, in a typical group, members presented eight different concerns. Although all members shared the common bond of distress, they had no common perspective or theme for addressing their issues.

When a common focus is not identified, group sessions may function like sequential individual sessions.

When a common focus is not identified, group sessions may function like sequential individual sessions. It appeared that we needed a guide that could assist us in defining focus areas.

In our search for this guide, we first assessed the topics our members presented. During approximately 9 months, we asked 39 members from six different groups to complete a brief questionnaire at the end of each group. Members were asked to write their re-

Table 2.2   Group Content Issues

Emotional and Cognitive Issues
    Anger, assertion, revenge
    "Child" within, "adolescent" within, parenting self
    Decision making, choices, goal attainment, taking risks
    Fear of progress, double binds
    Grief and loss issues, sadness
    Responsibility issues—blame, culpability of others, shame
    Spirituality and forgiveness
    Thought patterns—black and white thinking, negative self-talk

Social and Interpersonal Functioning Issues
    Family-of-origin issues—confrontation, protection of children
    Group issues—rules, roles, meaning of group, transference, needs, hugs,
        rivalry, congruence—am I what I present?
    Leader issues—power, safety, disappointments, offender is different now,
        rules and roles
    Parenting issues—current family system, current relationships
    Relationship issues—boundaries, giving and receiving, shared identity,
        idealizing others, not alone, feeling different, trust, betrayal, assessing
        others, trust of self
    Victimization—sexual assaults, domestic violence

Physical and Sexual Functioning Issues
    Physical symptoms, relaxation
    Sexuality issues—harassment, preferences, functioning

Compulsive Behaviors or Behaviors of Excess
    Addictions—chemical dependency, eating issues, "codependency"
    Self-care, enabling, wants and needs, spontaneity, personal freedom

Psychological Symptoms
    Anxieties, burn-out, feeling worse
    Depression, suicidal thoughts, hopelessness, helplessness
    Dissociative defenses, emotional defenses
    Flashbacks, new memories, numbing, PTSD symptoms

---

sponses to two questions: "What was most important for me regarding content?" and "What was most important for me regarding process?" Their responses were tabulated and organized according to symptom categories. They are summarized in Table 2.2.

Although we summarized 26 content areas from more than 90 topics, the result was too complex to provide a simple guide for therapists during group sessions. We looked to the literature on the long-term effects of incest for categorizations and noted that symptoms were categorized primarily for descriptive or diagnostic pur-

Table 2.3   The Power, Goodness, and Importance Model

Perspective	Therapeutic goal
Power	
Control	Empower choices
Hope	Encourage hope
Safety	Promote safety
Goodness	
Trust	Facilitate trust
Responsibility	Clarify responsibilities
Secrecy	Encourage openness
Importance	
Connection	Support healthy relationships
Significance	Illustrate significance
Identity	Clarify a positive identity

poses. Because we had difficulty applying those types of categorizations to the content issues presented in our groups, we devised a framework that categorizes issues and symptoms into three major themes: *power, goodness,* and *importance.* These categories appear to be simple enough for the therapist to keep in mind during a group session, but inclusive enough to address the complex needs and symptoms of incest survivors like those in our therapy groups. Within each of the broad categories of power, goodness, and importance are nine subcategories: the *power theme* organizes issues associated with control, hope, and safety; the *goodness theme* encompasses issues related to trust, responsibility, and secrecy; the *importance theme* refers to intimacy, self-worth, and identity issues (Table 2.3). (Since the conception of the PGI model, we have become aware of a cognitive model presented by McCann and Pearlman, 1990, that is applicable to trauma victims in general. These authors present a helpful organization of the major cognitive schemas related to the traumatization effects, many of which correspond to the cognitive themes subsumed in the PGI model.)

The PGI model allows the therapist to identify a common focus as well as a clinical approach for addressing that focus. It is not an empirical framework, but a guide to help organize the wealth of information presented during a group session. Once a theme is chosen for focus, members can either "stay in content" by analyzing related beliefs, emotions, and behavioral patterns, or "process" by exploring how that particular theme is reflected by the group's interactions. For example, in one group session, four members asked for time to discuss personal issues. One member discussed difficulties with a boss, two others talked about issues related to their mothers, and the fourth member discussed whether or not to confront her perpetrator. As the therapist assessed the divergent topics, she searched for a theme that could synthesize them. She chose to focus on the theme of power by saying, "As I hear each of you describe your issues, it seems they relate to the theme of power and control. I'm wondering how that theme relates to what you've all been discussing?" The group, having a common focus, then discussed how the theme of power related to their specific issues. In this instance, the therapist named a theme and invited members to comment on its applicability. Instead of naming the theme, the therapist could have chosen to focus on power by asking members to reflect on the process of the group. She may have said, "As I hear each of you describe your issues, I'm wondering how much power each of you feel within the group?"

The PGI model, like the 4 Ms, should assist the therapist in organizing her or his thoughts about what is happening in the group. By choosing a theme, the therapist helps the group focus on a common purpose ostensibly related to the effects of childhood abuse. Because all themes relate to the effects of abuse, exploring any theme should be beneficial in some way. Chapter 3 thoroughly discusses each theme and subtheme and the associated therapeutic actions.

CLIENT PREPARATION

Preparation for group begins with the first individual session. Clients typically begin the program by scheduling a minimum of three or four 50-minute sessions. If scheduling allows, the first session covers a double time slot (100 minutes). During this session the client is introduced to the program and assessment begins. The therapist strives to approach assessment in a supportive, nonjudgmental, and matter-of-fact manner. Individuals differ greatly in terms of their agendas and may or may not be comfortable about discussing the specifics of their abuse at this time. The therapist needs to allow for individual needs while imposing enough structure to keep the session safe and productive.

The assessment process includes the use of both informal information-gathering and formal standardized assessment tools. Informal assessment focuses on current life circumstances, day-to-day functioning, general symptomatology, social support, coping skills, level of distress, past or current therapy, reported diagnoses or issues, and goals in seeking therapy. A social history that includes information about the sexual abuse and its context, family of origin, and past coping patterns is also completed. Information regarding the abuse is summarized on a form organized according to Finkelhor and Browne's (1985) four traumagenic factors. Specific formal assessment tools that are completed in our program include the Beck Depression Inventory (Beck, 1978), the State-Trait Anxiety Inventory (Spielberger et al., 1968), and the Response to Childhood Incest Questionnaire (Edwards & Donaldson, 1989). We also recommend Briere's Trauma Symptom Checklist (Briere, 1989).

In addition to the assessments, the therapist provides general information about the short-term and long-term effects of childhood incest. The therapist discusses the importance of education and gives clients two segments of the Village's educational materials. A booklet, *Incest Years After: Putting the Pain to Rest* (Donaldson, 1983) defines incest, describes the nature of delayed stress responses and other effects, and recounts the reactions and feelings of clients in our early groups. An audiotape, *Incest Years After: A Lecture on Theory and Treatment* (Donaldson, 1986) reviews the nature of sexual abuse, post-traumatic stress disorder, and recovery from the aftereffects of childhood sexual abuse. Clients also receive literature that describes the programs and options that are available to them and to their significant others (e.g., the partners group).

Memory work allows the client to release emotions and reframe beliefs.

Subsequent individual sessions focus on memory work that allows clients to recount memories of past traumatic events. The client recounts in detail memories of the past abuse and describes the context in which it occurred. It is essential for her to understand how she, as a child, interpreted the abuse given the limitations of her knowledge, cognitive abilities, and support mechanisms. The therapist helps the client understand how the early learning experiences may have affected subsequent beliefs, emotions, and behavior. The goal of memory work is to allow the client to identify emotions related to the trauma and to reframe associated beliefs rationally. Memory work is often intensely emotional and can seem overwhelming for clients. When emotions become too intense, the therapist helps the client step back and focus on coping skills she has learned. (An audiotape, *Memory Work: Individual Therapy with Adult Incest Survivors* [Donaldson, 1988] offers an in-depth description of our memory work process.)

In addition to memory work, individual sessions provide supportive therapy in which anxiety, depression, post-traumatic stress disorder (PTSD), and general functioning issues are addressed. The therapist assists in the process of choosing options for continuing therapy.

Most of the clients who become involved in our incest treatment program present first for individual therapy but are aware that our program involves group work. Some are referred by outside individual therapists for group work alone. Certainly individual therapy alone will remain a viable option for some people and for some programs. However, because of the potential benefits group therapy can offer, we encourage our clients to take part in a group unless there are contraindications for doing so. (See Group Composition and Member Selection for a discussion of contraindications.) For most clients who choose to attend group at some time during their tenure in our program, group is the primary form of treatment. Clients who generally function at a high level and do not have a great need for individual support spend approximately 6 to 8 hours in initial individual therapy. Once they begin group, these clients schedule occasional sessions with their primary therapist to discuss any pertinent issues or to receive additional support or assessment as needed. Other group clients are seen individually on a twice weekly, weekly, biweekly, or monthly basis. The amount of time spent in individual sessions depends on the client's needs, available support systems, and severity of symptoms.

Education Groups

After the initial four or five individual sessions, most clients begin an education group. We believe that it is important for survivors to understand at the outset the basic issues involved in their past abuse. These issues may include factors that contribute to the occurrence of incest, typical consequences for individuals, typical effects on families, the child victim's coping strategies, and the typical course of recovery.

Many of these issues can be addressed as part of individual therapy; however, there are several advantages to an education group format. Therapists who work with a large number of survivors often find themselves repeating the same lectures over and over. Education groups can incorporate these lectures and save time and money for the program and clients alike. More time is available to focus on individual needs in the initial individual sessions.

Education groups may also serve as a form of desensitization because they provide a nonthreatening setting in which the individual first meets other survivors. Although members may hear information that is sometimes uncomfortable, they are instructed to simply take in the information and not be concerned about self-disclosure. Clients who complete education group may start a therapy group already sharing some basic understanding about issues that will be most common in the group. For all of these reasons, we encourage most of our clients in the incest treatment program to attend education groups. In cases where this is not feasible, or if a client already has an adequate grasp of pertinent issues, education group may be waived or may be included as needed as part of the individual sessions.

Education groups are conducted by therapists or graduate interns who are members of the incest treatment team. Our current program involves four weekly sessions of 1 ½ hours each. To help standardize the information given, we wrote *Incest Years After: Learning to Cope Successfully* (Donaldson & Cordes-Green, 1987). This workbook was designed specifically for use in our education group as well as by individuals. This book includes basic information on incest, self-assessment worksheets, and self-explorative exercises. It allows clients to assess their thoughts, feelings, and behaviors in regard to incest as they become familiar with information and issues pertinent to incest. Issues are illustrated through the eyes of four fictional women who are adult survivors of incest.

The education groups begin with clients introducing themselves by first names. Before embarking on the topic for the day, the therapist acknowledges that some may be feeling uncomfortable and reassures them that these feelings are normal and understandable. The therapist also informs members that they may feel a bit overwhelmed by the amount of new information that will be presented. They are encouraged to "take what they are ready to work with now, and stick the rest in their back pocket." The workbook is theirs to keep and to use as they become ready.

Basic rules for safety and confidentiality are outlined. (See Group Mechanics and General Information in this chapter for a complete description of group rules.) In addition to basic rules, we inform members that they are free to leave the room or ask the therapist for help if their stress level becomes overwhelming. Although self-assessment exercises are contained in the workbook, the leader encourages minimal discussion of the completed exercises and assures members that there will be ample time for open, personal exploration during the therapy groups. In this way, clients are educated about the effects of incest before they are expected to share vulnerable, personal information in a group setting. Each education group is built around a specific chapter from the workbook that covers a specific topic area. These topics are:

1. Why does incest happen? The impact of family and society.
2. What are the effects of Incest? Incest and stress.
3. Growth and change: What can you do to deal with the incest?
4. What can you do for yourself? Self-care.

Why does incest happen? The impact of family and society. In this session, we review the societal and familial context of the abuse. Members begin to understand that the context of the abuse may have been as damaging as the sexual abuse itself (Donaldson & Gardner, 1985). Issues such as stereotypical gender roles and power distributions within societal institutions (including the family) are explored. The societal issues may explain the larger context of abuse, but most survivors have specific questions about their own abuse. To help them understand the psychological and social issues that contributed to their perpetrator(s)' abusive behavior, we review Finklehor's (1984) four preconditions for the occurrence of familial sexual abuse. The leader explains the various motivations, the process of overcoming internal inhibitors, the process of overcoming external inhibitors, and how a child's resistance may be overcome. A thorough review of interpersonal boundaries follows this discussion. This review includes concepts of physical and emotional boundaries, healthy boundaries in relationships, and boundaries in their families of origin. In addition, we present information on family rules emphasizing those that perpetuate secrecy. Family roles are also assessed. We place special emphasis on victim and offender roles. Then we review power in the family system, which includes clarification of concepts such as homeostasis and power imbalances. Finally, we offer suggestions for coping with one's family of origin.

In addition to these discussions regarding family issues, we emphasize the importance of nonfamilial support systems. After healthy supportive relationships are defined, members assess their personal support system. The session closes with a review of affirmations regarding blame, power, roles, and support.

What are the effects of incest? Incest and stress. In this session, we review the relationship between stress and sexual victimization. A description of the responses of fight, flight, and freeze allows members to begin to identify their emotional and behavioral responses to the abuse. We discuss typical reactions to the actual abuse and assure members that physically pleasurable reactions to the abuse are common and do not imply compliance. The concept of secondary stressors (stressors occurring in the abusive context such as being near the offender, certain looks, sibling comments) is also reviewed. Recognizing secondary stressors may help members understand stress they experienced in childhood as well as in the present. To help them understand their childhood coping pattern, we review factors that affect children's coping. We explain that without protective factors (Garmezy, 1983), children may be more distressed and may develop characteristic patterns of coping (some of which may now be dysfunctional for them as adults). The theory of PTSD is described to help members understand the process of working through old stress. Because members may be experiencing symptoms such as flashbacks, dissociative episodes, body memories, anxiety, and depression, we provide an outline of suggestions for coping with PTSD-related symptoms. The session ends with a review of affirmations regarding coping with stress, balancing, using defenses, and giving oneself credit for coping.

Growth and change: What can you do to deal with the incest? This session introduces some concepts helpful in understanding the process of recovery. Members are introduced to concepts such as negative beliefs and cognitive restructuring, and begin to assess their basic beliefs. Members assess their commonly experienced emotions and are given tips about how to accept, cope, and work through them. Special emphasis is placed on the emotional and cognitive aspects of shame. The concept of psychological defenses is also discussed. Members may discover that many of their psychological defenses have been helpful in coping with the abusive past. They are encouraged to view their defenses as their friends, not their captors. For example, many members feel helpless regarding dissociative defenses. When they begin to understand the adaptive function of dissociation, they may also understand that they can develop some control over dissociative reactions. Behavioral patterns, especially victim-like behavior, are also examined. Many members have never evaluated their behavioral patterns and find this a helpful step in changing patterns that are dysfunctional. As with the other sessions, affirmations are presented. The focus is on recovery, reframing beliefs, emotional release, and behavioral change.

What can you do for yourself? Self-care. This session begins with a self-assessment regarding physical, emotional, social, and spiritual needs. Physical needs are reviewed. Topics such as body image, nutrition, exercise, and relaxation are highlighted. Members are given practical tips about simple relaxation techniques, including controlled breathing and progressive muscle relaxation. Sexuality issues, including information on sexual dysfunctions and personal choice regarding intimacy, are presented. As emotional needs are explored, the concept of the "child within" is introduced. Intellectual self-care is described as "mind development" and self-improvement. Social needs are also explored. The importance of friends, family, play, and therapy is emphasized. We discuss the importance of the members learning to balance their needs with others. Spiritual issues are introduced and members are encouraged to think about their concepts regarding spirituality. The affirmations in this session center on developing positive beliefs regarding self-care.

❏ The Formation Stage of Group

During the formation stage of group, the therapist makes final decisions about membership, time, and location. Then the therapist contacts members and asks them to make a commitment to the group.

GROUP COMPOSITION
AND MEMBER SELECTION

If decisions regarding the format, number of members, number of sessions, and duration of the group have not been made previously, they need to be made at this time. In our program, groups consist of six to eight members who make an initial commitment of 6 months. In making selections, the therapist should consider the ideal group composition. Yalom (1985) suggests that a long-term intensive therapy group should encompass "heterogeneity for conflict areas, and homogeneity for ego strength" (p. 265), balanced for factors such as sexual orientation, affective expression, insight, passiveness versus aggression, and age.

Although such guidelines are helpful, in reality factors such as scheduling, economics, space, and availability of leaders or members often play the greatest role in determining a group's composition. As a consequence, group composition is seldom ideal. Even if we had power to create an ideal group, much of its success would depend on factors that are hard to predict. We try as much as possible to select members in such a way as to avoid major problems that could potentially hinder the effectiveness of a group, and attempt to achieve a balance of individual strengths and characteristics.

The major factors we consider in making selections of potential members for group are age, severity of abuse, symptomatology, social skills, willingness/readiness, offending behavior, sexual orientation, and commitment.

Age

Clients sometimes express concern that other members will be much older or younger. However, willingness to participate actively is more likely to be a salient factor than age alone. There are some benefits to age heterogeneity as long as the age differences are not too extreme. Age differences often seem to help bring about resolution of parent/child issues in a healthy working group. As one middle-aged woman stated to a college-age woman in group, "Well, I guess if you can understand my feelings, my daughter can too." The younger woman replied, "Thanks! You've helped me understand how hard my mom's role was—how it might have been hard for her to protect me."

Type or Severity of Abuse

Because family-of-origin issues are central to the therapy group, we include in our groups only those who were abused by a family member (parent, uncle, grandparent, brother, sister) or by a person in a familial-type role (mom's live-in boyfriend or a close family friend who spent a great deal of time in the home). The deciding factor is whether or not the individual should have held a position of trust and should have been nurturing or protective toward the victim. Although type, severity, and age may be factors in the long-term consequences, most findings (see chapter 1) indicate that most incest has the potential to damage and the consequences to survivors are legitimate and worth addressing regardless of the details of the victimization. Therefore we include in our groups those clients with a somewhat limited memory of their victimization as well as those with clear memories. Frequently, group members will begin to recall abusive events which they did not report at the outset (Courtois, 1992). Several clients in our groups have reported that they have found convincing evidence, such as the reports of friends or relatives or school and medical records, which have corroborated memories which had been seemingly repressed or forgotten. However, recent research (Loftus, 1993) has questioned the nature of concepts such as memory repression and has also suggested that an indivdual's recall of past events may be influenced by therapists and others. Until such time as concepts such as repression, amnesia, and dissociation are better defined, we must continue to behave responsibly by refraining from suggesting the possible existence of memories unless the client questions these or there is some existing evidence. Our job is not to act as judge and jury, but to support members in working through their experiences. If a group member is not a legitimate victim, she is not likely to identify with other members and may drop out of group early.

Symptomatology

Group members generally have a wide range of behaviors and vary considerably in terms of the intensity of their symptoms. Many are somewhat depressed or anxious as group begins. Usually, it is best to exclude persons who are profoundly depressed, actively psychotic, consistently a danger to themselves or others, actively using chemical substances, or need more consistent support and therapy or lack essential back-up support.

Social and Cognitive Skills

We may exclude clients so lacking in social skills or empathic ability that they are unable to respond, to communicate, or to achieve any degree of insight. However, we have at times set up a special group for those deficient in social skills. This group utilizes a behavioral format to improve these skills as well as general functioning. Some of the "graduates" of this group have later gone on to become active and vital group members who benefited greatly in a regular therapy group.

Willingness and Readiness

As a general rule, clients who are extremely anxious about group or are unable to commit in terms of time and effort will not benefit from the experience. Involuntary clients (such as those who were referred by a court or coerced in some way) may do well only if they begin to derive some intrinsic value from the group.

Abusive Behavior

At times, persons who have been accused or convicted of acts of violence such as child abuse are referred to our groups. Clients who are current or past offenders, especially those who refuse to "own" their own abusiveness, will likely elicit extreme reactions from the group. To exclude such a person or not is a matter of judgment. If the offending member is motivated to change her offending behavior and is willing to discuss with the group her past abusive behavior, she may join a group. She is, however, informed that other members may have strong reactions to her past offending behavior. We have had situations in which members such as these have admitted to their offending behavior, accepted the group's confrontation, and went on to become valuable group members. In these situations other group members reported that they felt safe and more powerful as a result of having confronted this person. We have also had situations in which the offending member denied or minimized her abusive behavior and the results for the group were disastrous. Other members could not feel safe and the offending member left the group.

Sexual Orientation

As a rule, we view sexual orientation as a reason for neither inclusion nor exclusion. A homosexual client's "coming out" in group may be uncomfortable for either her or some group members, but may offer excellent growth opportunities for all members of the group. To be openly accepted by heterosexual women may mean a great deal to a lesbian woman who has been secretive about her sexual preferences. Heterosexual members may benefit from learning about the gay lifestyle.

Commitment

After group members are screened and an initial member list put together, members are contacted and asked if they are able to commit to the group for at least 6 months. After 6 months, clients may then choose whether or not to renew depending on their progress. Clients may have varying reactions at this point. Some are initially confident but become very anxious when asked to make a commitment. If they do not express this anxiety openly, they may become "no shows" for group. Therefore, it is helpful to open the way for a discussion of ambivalence prior to the point of commitment to a group.

❏ The Pretherapy Group

Pretherapy group provides information regarding the therapist's and clients' roles in group, expectations, and group mechanics, and emphasizes skills training and goal setting. The pretherapy, or preparation, group can be considered the first phase of group. If the therapist has assumed the role of a teacher or an individual therapist, she or he will need to expand her or his thoughts and behaviors to fit with the role of group therapist.

Clients likewise need to learn how to become active members of a group. They need to understand how the group therapy experience will differ from individual therapy or from other types of groups in which they may have participated in the past. Because it is difficult for the client to comprehend fully what a group experience will be like in advance, it may seem a bit mysterious. Pregroup training dispels this sense of mystery by informing members about what to expect from the therapist, themselves, and other members by giving them specific tools that will allow them to achieve their goals in group.

The pretherapy group is topic centered and examines four main areas:

1. what to expect during therapy group,
2. roles of the therapist and members,
3. skills training,
4. group mechanics.

Because this group is partially didactic, the therapist is fairly directive but encourages increasing client participation as the group progresses. As a general rule, clients who began pretherapy group together are preselected as a therapy group, and will continue on together in their therapy. Our pretherapy group is in some ways similar to the Education Phase format described by Drews and Bradley (1989).

OVERVIEW OF PRETHERAPY GROUP TOPICS

What to Expect During Group Therapy

A variety of general issues is discussed in the first pretherapy session. One important concept is to clarify the difference between therapy and support and self-help groups. We describe therapy as "remodeling" and support/self-help as "redecorating." When one remodels a house, the basic structure of the house is changed by putting in windows or doors, removing walls, or adding rooms. In redecorating, the basic structure remains, but by painting or buying furniture, the living quarters are improved. We tell our clients that the goal of an incest therapy group is to change some "basic structures" within themselves by changing basic beliefs, resolving emotional distress, and enacting new behaviors. We also describe how the group can be helpful from session to session by highlighting Schulman's (1979) description of the group as a "mutual aid" system, in which the group functions through individuals helping one another.

> *Group members frequently ask, "Just what am I supposed to do in group?"*

What to Expect from the Therapist

The more defined the therapist's role, the more clearly members will be able to perceive their own roles. When the therapist's role is clear, the group will expend less time and energy negotiating it. To clarify the therapist's roles, we review for clients the 4 Ms and the PGI model. Members then can understand why the therapist is watching them, why and how the therapist intervenes, and the purpose of education breaks. Although members are encouraged to present topics that seem pertinent to them, they will be prepared for the therapist to elaborate on the thematic content of their discussions by highlighting power, goodness, and importance themes.

The Role of Members

Group members frequently ask, "Just what am I supposed to do in group?" This question is natural and may be asked for several reasons. Some fear that they will behave inappropriately or that others will confront them harshly. Others wish to be assured that they positively utilize the group experience. A few are anxious because they have misconceptions as a result of television shows or hearsay. These concerns may be allayed by giving clients an easy-to-follow guide that suggests productive group behaviors. The idea is not to present a performance standard, but to offer a way to learn and discuss basic behaviors. We introduce another mnemonic called the **4 Rs**—respect, reflect, respond, and receive. The 4 Rs are summarized in Table 2.4.

The 4 Rs. The 4 Rs were formulated to enable group members to remember appropriate behavior in group. The four categories are not necessarily all-inclusive, but do represent general categories of group behavior that should improve overall communication skills, empathic responding, personal responsibility, safety, and the definition of appropriate interpersonal boundaries. Most importantly, instead of focusing on "don'ts" or leaving the individual to flounder aimlessly, the 4 Rs teach what is helpful. They allow the therapist to be less directive because members have a "tool kit" to pull out as situations arise in group. This should allow members to respond more often and with greater confidence.

Respect. We believe that respect for self as well as for others is an essential element in an effective group. Respectful behavior allows individuals within the group to value and assert themselves without infringing on the rights of others. For those who grew up in families where mutual respect was not practiced, the experience of respect in group may be a corrective experience.

Mutual respect within the context of the group means that all members are equal in terms of needs and rights, all have a right to use the group experience to meet these needs, and members can differ in terms of opinions, experiences, and feelings and will still be respected. Although these guidelines seem commonsensical (if not a

Table 2.4   The 4 Rs for Group Members

Respect

    Consider the right of all to use the group experience to have their needs met in their own way.

    Respect the feelings and opinions of other group members, even if they differ from your own.

    Share the time with everyone, each has a valid need.

    Permit various opinions including your own.

    Cooperate with boundaries such as time, leader role, rules.

    View other members as helpful.

    Consider how the group as a whole is a healing force.

    Accept full membership in the group process.

    Promote safety at all times.

Reflect

    Listen carefully and think about what you are hearing.

    Try to put yourself in the place of the person who is sharing.

    Reflect upon your own thoughts and feelings.

    Compare your reaction to others' reactions.

    Consider different ways you would react.

    Evaluate how this experience may fit with your family of origin.

    Understand how you are important to the group experience.

Respond

    Let the person sharing know you are trying to understand.

    Offer your thoughts, ideas, relevant experiences, empathy, praise as fits the topic.

    If you are not sure how to respond in a helpful way, simply ask.

    Tell others what they have shared has meant to you.

    Offer your thoughts, ideas, relevant experiences.

    Share your own issues—even vulnerable ones.

    Reveal how you are changing your views of yourself.

Receive

    Express your thoughts, feelings, and needs; this is the first step to receiving help and support.

    Try to accept the responses you get from others with an open mind—consider suggestions carefully before accepting or discarding them.

    Remember you have a right to receive from others. Group works through give-and-take.

    Experience the caring from others.

    Let others know how you are receiving their support.

    Allow yourself to feel close to others.

---

bit idealistic), persons with a history of victimization may find them difficult to grasp and put into practice. For some, simply voicing a difference of opinion is quite threatening.

Reflect. Reflection skills are communication skills that involve listening and thinking through what is heard. These skills include attentive listening, taking the other person's perspective, and developing an awareness of one's own responses to the information that is shared. We often explore these skills by asking questions such as:

1. What did you hear?
2. How do you think she felt?
3. Have you ever felt like that?
4. Could different people in the group, depending on their point of view, hear that message in different ways?
5. How did that information affect you?

The last question is very important because incest survivors may have a difficult time sorting out ownership of feelings and thoughts. Even seemingly off-hand questions can trigger powerful reactions in other group members. Separating one's own feelings from others is an important skill for group members to learn.

Respond. Responding is sometimes the most difficult skill category for our clients. Often, when we ask a speaker what she needs, she will reply, "Just to know that you heard and understood." Sometimes all that others need to do is to reassure the speaker that they have heard her. Members can always ask the speaker what kind of response may be helpful. We also inform them that silences often occur in group for a variety of reasons and can be either a positive or a negative part of the group process.

Receive. People who learned to place others' needs first or have not had their own basic needs met may experience difficulty in learning to receive. Some will drain the group's resources in an attempt to have their own needs met; others will sit back quietly, afraid of "imposing," or will talk only if they are helping another. Group members need to understand that group is a give-and-take process in which all have the right to be the recipient as well as the benefactor. This will not always occur on an equal basis in a given session, but it tends to work out to everyone's satisfaction over the course of time if problems regarding the use of time can be dealt with openly.

Because individual needs and rates of progress vary, communication addressing needs and the level of satisfaction regarding those needs is essential.

As recipients in group, members are encouraged to express their own thoughts and feelings and to ask for help and support. Feedback from others should be considered with an open mind. Each individual decides for herself what to do in response to feedback. Some group members frequently need to be reminded that they have a right to the group's time and resources. As the group matures, more outgoing members may begin to draw out the more hesitant ones. This is especially true after the group members develop a genuine caring for one another.

SPECIFIC SKILLS TRAINING FOR MEMBERS

In addition to reviewing the 4 Rs, the skills training format involves education, modeling, practice (usually role playing), feedback, and homework. Clients learn, observe, and practice specific skills such as giving positive and negative feedback, listening and responding with empathy, asking for clarification, using "I messages," making assertive statements (discriminating between assertive and aggressive behavior), and maintaining individual boundaries. Occasionally the therapist chooses to offer an assertion training program.

Although we at the Village have not yet systematically studied the impact of the skills training component, the general consensus of the staff and clients alike is that this training makes a noticeable difference later in group. As a general rule, better trained groups seem to progress more quickly than less trained groups and seem to be able to negotiate problems better when they surface.

GROUP MECHANICS
AND GENERAL INFORMATION

Systems

In addition to specific skills training, members in pregroup receive information on systems theory. They learn about the unique characteristics of systems, how members in systems affect one another, and how rules and roles function in systems. They also learn the characteristics of healthy functioning systems, how to maintain appropriate boundaries, and how to deal with power imbalances in systems. Examples of typical family and group systems are presented. Members consider ways in which their past experiences and roles in other systems may influence their behaviors in group.

Content Versus Process

Pregroup members are educated about the difference between content and process issues in group. We define content as "what is said" and process as "how and why it is said." Members learn why process is as important to the group as content and that discussion of process issues often merits use of the group's time even when members are eager to use the group time individually. The therapist presents an overview of the development of a typical therapy group, and highlights content and process issues as they occur through the stages of development.

Goal Setting

Members work together to help each person set reasonable goals for group. This becomes a step-by-step process in which members first define the problems that brought them to group. Once problems are listed, members are asked to describe the desired outcomes or goals for each problem. As members clarify their goals, the leader presents examples of reasonable and unreasonable goals, and highlights the need for specificity and flexibility in setting goals. An example of an unreasonable goal might be, "I want to feel completely comfortable with sex by the time group is over." A reasonable goal might be, "I want to able, by the end of this month, to discuss my feelings about sex with my husband." After reasonable goals are delineated, each member explores ways in which the group may be helpful in achieving goals. Throughout this process, goals are continually refined and become increasingly specific. As members list their goals, the therapist may wish to categorize them within the PGI framework.

Group Mechanics

Discussions addressing group mechanics focus on rules and norms that will govern the functioning of the group. Members are reminded that assurance of safety, trust, and the right to utilize resources is the primary function of group rules. Some of the group rules are arbitrary; other rules are decided by the group via the democratic process.

Consistent rules and norms. Rules that are consistent cover the following issues:

- Confidentiality
- Attendance and commitment
- Use of psychoactive substances
- Verbal and physical abuse
- Touching
- Outside contacts

1. Confidentiality: Group participants are expected to maintain strict confidentiality regarding the identity of participants and the issues they discuss in the group. The leader may need to identify situations in which potential problems with confidentiality may occur and help the members plan for ways to deal with those. Members may be asked if they would like to be greeted or acknowledged should others encounter them outside the group setting (e.g., seeing them in the local mall or at a concert).

2. Attendance and commitment: Members are reminded of their commitment to the group (usually 6 months) and of the need to notify the agency should they be unable to attend a particular session. They are also reminded that, should they choose or be forced to leave the group at some time prior to its closing, they are expected to follow through with closure. Commitment also involves accepting responsibility in paying for services. Members who are in arrears with their fees may be asked to terminate.

3. Use of psychoactive substances: Members may not participate in group if they are under the influence of drugs, alcohol, solvent fumes, or the like. A member who arrives for group intoxicated will be asked to leave and may not return for future sessions unless she arrives sober.

4. Verbal or physical abuse: Physical or verbal attacks are prohibited. Groups may need assistance in determining whether certain types of verbal confrontations should be termed "attacks."

5. Touching: With the exception of a handshake, no member may touch another without that person's prior consent. This rule is intended to protect members who may experience adverse reactions to certain types of touching. For some members, feeling compelled to participate in activities such as a group hug may be anxiety inducing or may trigger flashbacks.

6. Outside contacts: Although we recognize that this is a "free country," we insist that group members report to the group any contact they have with one another outside group sessions. This rule attempts to prevent the establishment of unhealthy alliances that can result in covert subgrouping.

Negotiable rules and norms. Each group decides whether or not it will allow smoking, take breaks, and exchange phone numbers. Groups also may make decisions about certain aspects of the use of time and resources. These decisions include how the group will be opened and closed, how it will make decisions about sharing time when demand is high, how it will handle tardiness or departing during a session, and how many absences will be allowed. Specific requests will also be negotiated, for example, when a certain member requests a no cursing rule. The leader facilitates the democratic process but provides advice or feedback based on her or his experiences with group. The leader makes it clear to the group that she or he will intervene if the group adopts norms that threaten either individual members' rights or the integrity of the group.

3

Working With Content Issues

Effective leaders of therapy groups must attend to both content and process issues. Although both occur simultaneously, they are described separately for the purpose of organization. This chapter focuses on content issues from the perspectives of Power, Goodness and Importance (PGI) as outlined in Chapter 2. Applying the PGI perspectives to issues presented by group members should assist the therapist in focusing on dynamics related to incest. Some issues, such as confrontation of the offender or concerns regarding sexuality, may be viewed from all of the perspectives. For example, confronting the offender may be viewed from the Power/Control Perspective if the member is seeking to regain power. Or it may be viewed from the Importance/Connection Perspective if the member is seeking to clarify her relationship with the offender. Keep in mind that the "correctness" of the therapist's choice of a particular perspective is not as important as guiding the group members to focus on a common theme.

To illustrate the applications of this framework, we introduce a fictional therapy group that will be discussed in this and the next chapter.

66

Although the names and specifics of this group are fictional, the content and processes reflected are based on actual group experience.

> The group members are Twyla, Angie, Kate, Dorie, and Ann. Twyla, a 43-year-old divorced mother of two grown daughters, is a sales clerk and part-time social work student. Her father and brother, whom she describes as "lower than low," sexually abused her for about six years. She tends to be quite controlling and highly intellectual. Although she readily acknowledges her controlling behavior as a problem, she feels helpless to change it. Angie is a single 22-year-old college drop out who is working at a fast food restaurant. She was a victim of extensive physical and sexual abuse by her father, her uncles, and her grandfather. Angie, chemically dependent but sober for one year, is guarded and withdraws from emotionally intimate interactions. She is frightened that the "new memories" coming forth will further disrupt "the chaos that is me." Kate is a 27-year-old mother of three toddlers who is married to "the most wonderful man in the world." Although trained as a nurse, she has chosen to remain at home with her children. She was raised by a "devoted and caring family." Her father, the offender and a retired minister, is a regular visitor in Kate's home. Dorie, a 32-year-old married bank executive, was referred to the group because of her persistent, unexplained headaches. She is childless and describes her life as "one big whirlwind." Although she acknowledges the sexual abuse by her grandfather as "something that messed up my childhood," she denies its current impact. Ann, whose brother sexually abused her for most of her childhood, is a 33-year-old divorced mother of two children. She is clinically depressed and has been taking antidepressants for two years. Although she agreed to attend the therapy group, she is frightened that "they will attack me just like the last group." In the past, Ann had attended a growth group in which members were often confronted in a harsh manner.

❏ The Power Perspective

Finkelhor and Browne (1985) refer to the powerlessness experienced with sexual abuse as "the process in which the child's wills, desires, and sense of efficacy are continually contravened" (p. 532). Children, because of their status, do not have the power to resist the abuse or alter the abusive environment. Even if status is equalized, as in some sibling abuse, victims often recall the feeling of being overpowered by the situation. This disempowerment is apparent when victims, as adults, believe and act as if they have little or no personal power (Jehu, 1988).

The perspective of power is categorized into three subthemes: control, hope and safety. Group members often report that they feel of little control over external circumstances or internal urges. Depression and anxiety are also commonly discussed. When viewed from the perspective of power, depression relates to the hopelessness, helplessness, and sadness related to the member's incestuous past. Members may also express fears about their safety as well as the safety of their children.

> During sessions 7 through 15, Twyla discussed feeling controlled by her boss (a man) and her subsequent "over-control" of her daughters. Angie often joined Twyla in discussing "men who always need to be right." She also expressed sadness about "growing up at age five." Kate, who "had the best husband anyone could want," would defend men, but also talked about her need to be more separate from her father. Dorie puzzled over discussions about controlling others and said, "You can't control other people so why worry about it. I'm more worried about my headaches." She often referred to the headaches as the "tormentor within." Ann could identify with Dorie's internal tormentor. Ann often talked about her depression and suicidal urges.
>
> During session 10, Angie revealed that her boyfriend had recently sexually assaulted her. She had become so angry with him that she started going to bars to try "picking up some jerk and then dumping him, just so he'd know what it feels like." Kate was quite upset about Angie's "pick-ups" and told her, "What you're doing is wrong both for yourself and for the man." Angie responded with, "What's wrong is your father being at your house all the time. How are you protecting your kids from him?" Kate, who was originally optimistic about the group, began to question whether therapy was making things worse, especially because Angie had "attacked her." Others discussed Angie's assault and her reactive behavior toward men. Twyla discussed her fear of being assaulted and made a decision to withdraw from men. As Ann recalled being raped during her senior year of high school, she became more depressed. She began having frequent flashbacks of that rape and her childhood incest. Ann would often make comments like, "I feel like I did when I was little, there seems to be no escape except death."

THE SUBTHEME OF CONTROL

Many adults who have been physically or emotionally abused in relationships seem to accept victimization as their role. As Swink and Leveille (1986) state, "these women often do not recognize this behavior as out of the ordinary, or as preventable" (p.126). Many members describe this behavior and express feeling powerless over relationships with bosses, coworkers, spouses or parents. A few, like Twyla, may present a facade of power and even intimidate others. Although they learn to project an image of power, they often feel like impostors (Courtois, 1988).

In addition to feeling powerless over external circumstances, many feel equally as powerless over emotions or symptoms. Some discuss loss of control over drinking, eating, spending, gambling, or sexual behavior. As reported in Chapter 1, various addictive or compulsive disorders may be related to childhood incest. From the perspective of power, these addictive behaviors may be framed as a loss of control over thoughts or urges. When members experience nightmares, flashbacks, intrusive thoughts, emotional numbness, denial, and dissociative episodes regarding the sexual abuse (Donaldson & Gardner, 1985; Courtois, 1992; Braun, 1989), these PTSD symptoms may also be framed as an internal loss of control.

Members may discuss experiencing a lack of both external and internal control in regard to sexual interactions and sexual responsiveness. Many believe they have no choice but to engage in sexual behavior if someone else desires it. They even discuss feeling guilty if they cannot respond to their partner. Others experience control in regards to external pressures, but may be distressed by an inner lack of control. They may be bothered by flashbacks during sexual closeness, may lack desire, or may experience physical numbness.

In addition to addressing current power and control issues, members also discuss their experiences of powerlessness during childhood. Many members were physically and emotionally abused as well as sexually abused and also may have witnessed the abuse of others. They may have learned to cope and accommodate to this abusive environment by acknowledging their helplessness and reacting passively to others (Summit, 1983). Some report that, although they had little control over the abuse, they experienced a sense of power because they protected others. They may say, "If I hadn't been the victim, I knew it would be my sister. At least I did something to help someone else." These members are especially distressed if they discover their younger siblings were abused despite their efforts to prevent it. A few discuss the abuse as if they did have control over its occurrence, and they excuse the offender(s) of his or her culpability. These members appear more willing to admit to the shame of being responsible rather than acknowledging their powerlessness.

Therapeutic Goal: Empower Choices

Cognitive/Behavioral Issues. The therapist may take a cognitive approach by asking members to discuss their beliefs about choices and relate those beliefs to the incest. For example, Kate stated that she believed that she should never allow her needs to take priority over others' needs. As a result of group feedback, Kate realized that this belief encouraged her to place her father's needs above her own. Through this type of analysis, members may realize that the beliefs which assisted their accommodation to their abuse are now handicaps to them as adults (Summit, 1983). They may also realize that many of their beliefs are distorted. For example, many survivors struggle with dichotomous thinking or "all-or-nothing" beliefs (Jehu, 1988; Briere, 1989). Therefore, members may believe they have all of the control or none of it. As members change their beliefs regarding control and choice, they allow themselves to acknowledge and exercise their personal power. As they do this, however, they may also experience ambivalence. Some fear that if they feel powerful they will become abusive. In this case, members may be helped to understand that to experience a sense of personal power does not mean they must behave in overtly controlling ways. Others fear that if they acknowledge their power, they will then be totally responsible for themselves and others. To address this, the group may discuss degrees of power and responsibility. For example, Twyla was encouraged to understand the limits of her power within her job and then assert herself within those limits. Likewise, Kate was encouraged to view her responsibility toward the caring of her children as shared by her husband and other caregivers.

Ambivalence regarding control also becomes apparent when group members discuss sexuality and choice. Some want a close sexual relationship but are frightened about losing control over their sexual responsiveness. Some fear becoming "oversexed" or promiscuous. Others fear that if they say "yes" to their partner's sexual advance once, they cannot say "no" the next time. Members should be informed that taking control over their sexual behavior is essential to their sexual healing (Maltz & Holman, 1987). As adults, they can now control whether a sexual interaction takes place and the pace of that interaction. They may also realize that they can take control of their behavior even when they are sexually aroused.

The therapist affirms her or his belief in giving members control by refusing to make choices for them within the group. When members look for direction, the therapist may say, "I think you should ask the group about that." or "What would you like to do?" Hesitant or nonparticipating members, like Dorie, may be encouraged to practice making choices by assertively asking for time within the group. Aggressive members, like Twyla, may be encouraged to practice assertion and respect. Members may also assist each other in analyzing the choices they have, both within group and in their everyday lives. As they analyze these choices, they can highlight for each other the choices they do have, and they can reinforce each other for the positive choices they make.

Brickman (1984) and Cole (1985) advocate that incest should be conceptualized from a feminist perspective. This perspective recognizes the validity of women's experiences within a societal structure in which there are institutionalized imbalances of power. As members discuss their experiences within various systems and structures, they may be challenged to examine their beliefs about female roles. Members may ask, "Why am I responsible for the housework when I work full-time just like my husband?" or " Why should I have to live with lewd comments at work?" Through this discovery process, members may feel empowered to adopt new beliefs about sexuality, careers, relationships, and other women's issues.

Emotional Issues. The therapist may focus on aspects of internal control and choice by presenting information in regard to identifying, expressing, and containing emotions. As members discuss their childhoods, they may experience emotions such as fear, anxiety, anger, shame and sadness. Many, however, are frightened about losing control over their emotions. Members, like Ann, may need to practice moving in and out of emotions related to flashbacks (Donaldson & Gardner, 1985). Others, like Twyla, may be encouraged to recognize and reveal a range of emotions other than anger. The group could be asked to "see through Twyla's anger" so she can reveal her vulnerability. Members who struggle with addictive/compulsive behaviors may be asked to explore the related emotions. As the leader encourages members to experience their emotions, for brief periods, within the safety of a group, they may realize that they can experience emotions without being overwhelmed or behaving destructively.

THE SUBTHEME OF HOPE

Many group members recall experiencing a pervasive hopelessness during their childhood. Some may recall that they prayed to die. As adults, some may continue to see dying as their only hope of escaping the pain of the abuse. These types of members may be described as suffering from a "disorder of hope" (van der Kolk, 1987). They feel despair about their future and feel helpless to make choices that positively influence their life. Although their childhood despair may have accurately reflected the reality of their lives then, the same outlook may not be applicable to their lives now as adults. As members are challenged to adopt more optimistic views, some defend their pessimistic outlook as being a practical way to prepare for the negative experiences that are certain to occur. They may even have difficulty imagining hopeful outcomes because they question, "Why build hopes only to have them dashed?"

Many feel hopeless about having good relationships with their families of origin. They may have accepted the reality of their family's dysfunction but have become so hopeless about family relationships that they overlook possible avenues for support or connection when they do exist. Conversely, others may be unrealistically hopeful. For example, Kate refuses to acknowledge negative aspects about family relationships and circumstances. She either reframes abusive behavior as caring behavior ("I know my dad tries to show me he cares when he criticizes me.") or clings to the hope of transforming them ("If I'm patient and loving he'll change.")

Obviously, such feelings of hopelessness are strongly tied to depression. Depression is frequently experienced by sexual abuse survivors (see Chapter 1) and is commonly discussed in group. Many members report feeling helpless and hopeless about many aspects of their lives. Some, like Ann, who are seriously depressed, regularly discuss suicide. Others may describe bouts of depression and describe their life as being like a roller coaster. They fear that they will never experience stability.

Therapeutic Goal: Encourage Hope

Cognitive/Behavioral Issues. The therapist might intervene cognitively by assisting members in discovering their mental filtering (Jehu, 1988) or negative beliefs (Beck, 1976). Members may help each other realize how frequently they concentrate on negatives and ignore positive aspects of situations. Members could then be encouraged to look for positive and hopeful aspects of situations. For example, the therapist could say to Ann, "I am hearing your hopelessness and pain, but I would like you to state one positive way you could influence your present situation." If Ann has difficulty doing this, the therapist could enlist the help of other group members. Members may also be encouraged to analyze circumstances from both positive and negative perspectives. For example, Kate could be gently encouraged to look at the negative aspects of her relationship with her father. In this way, the group can help members see things objectively without framing their situation as either completely negative or positive.

The leader and members can reinforce behaviors that lead to positive outcomes such as making new friends, taking classes, contacting positive family members, etc. Feedback can also help members change negative behaviors which contribute to feelings of hopelessness.

The leader should continually strive to enhance a hopeful group atmosphere. If members do not experience hope about the group's potential helpfulness, they will not commit the energy needed for the group to be effective. Members, like Kate, may need frequent assurance that things "often seem worse before they get better." To highlight hope, some groups end each meeting on a hopeful note.

Emotional Issues. The therapist may address the emotional aspect of this subtheme by encouraging members to grieve. As members express their grief, the leader should encourage them to acknowledge the sadness of loss as well as the hope for new beginnings (Axelroth, 1991). Members should be informed that the grief process varies in intensity and may occur over a long period of time. As they grieve, they will likely discuss how the abuse robbed them of their childhood. Grieving is difficult for both those experiencing the grief and those witnessing it. To assess the impact of members' grief, the leader may ask questions such as "What was it like for you to see Ann cry as she just did?" This type of process question encourages members to respond to the one grieving and allows the leader to assess how members are coping with the intensity of emotion.

THE SUBTHEME OF SAFETY

It is not unusual for members in incest therapy groups to discuss sexual assaults besides the incest. As adults, many incest survivors have been battered or raped (Goodwin et al., 1990; Armsworth, 1989). Many victims are unable to discern whether other people are potentially abusive and are unable to defend themselves if danger is threatened. When a group member, like Angie, is sexually assaulted, the entire group must face the fact that they too are potential victims.

As children, many were sexually abused by multiple perpetrators, physically and emotionally abused by their mothers, and/or psychologically abused by classmates and those in authority (Long & Jackson, 1991; Armsworth, 1989). As a result of this pervasive abuse, many survivors learned to be hypervigilant as children (Briere, 1992a). They would vigilantly watch the offender(s), to try to discern when an abusive incident would occur. Unfortunately, such alertness often does not prevent further victimization. A pattern of hypervigilance may continue into adulthood. Unfortunately, some incest survivors may perceive themselves to be at risk when little risk is present. For example, a friendly offer of lunch may be perceived as a potentially hurtful experience. Others do not perceive risk when it is present. They may deny another person's abusive potential even when it should be apparent. At times they may entrust their care, as well as the care of their children, to potentially abusive people (Brandt, 1989). A few, like Angie, engage in high risk behaviors. They may involve themselves in high risk situations to reverse the role of victim and offender. If they succeed in hurting someone else, however, they may feel empty and guilty rather than powerful.

Therapeutic Goal: Promote Safety

Cognitive/Behavioral Issues. Members can be helped to rationally and realistically assess safety issues. For example, if a member discusses a recent assault, the therapist should address ongoing physical safety. Questions to be explored include: "Is the offender still a threat?"; "Are there medical and legal interventions needed?"; or "Does their living situation minimize risks?" Members may discuss their views about personal safety and analyze how those views promote or limit self-protection. They could, as a group, analyze the safety of each other's relationships and living situations. Because some people are oblivious to dangerous situations, intermember feedback is crucial to these discussions. The leader should promote discussions of realistic precautions without reinforcing overly cautious self-protection.

In addition to protecting themselves from others, members may also need to consider how safe they are within themselves. The group may help them to identify belief patterns which may lead to self-destructive behavior. Through group feedback, they may also discover destructive thought patterns of which they have been unaware. For example, through group feedback, Ann identified a pattern of negative thoughts that conveyed that suicide was her only way out. Group members encouraged Ann to consider alternative beliefs. Because Ann discussed suicide often, she was encouraged to devise a safety plan in consultation with her individual therapist. (See Chapter 5 for further discussion of suicidal members.) Likewise, the group pointed out to Angie that she often said, "Some day I'll show them." Angie then realized how beliefs related to "showing others how powerful she is" influenced her to behave aggressively.

The leader encouraged members to help Angie adopt alternative views.

Emotional Issues. Members should be encouraged to experience and express emotions related to victimization such as fear, anxiety, shame, and loss. Although a member who was assaulted must experience her own pain, she can be comforted by the support of the other group members. As other members empathize with the victim, they may be reminded of their own past victimizations. The group setting may offer them an opportunity to work through their own past assaults.

❏ The Goodness Perspective

The perspective of goodness focuses on survivors' evaluations of their basic goodness. Many of our group members view themselves as being bad or even evil people. They believe that something is wrong with them that makes them tainted and unlovable. According to Finkelhor and Browne (1985), this self-evaluation maybe the result of stigmatization associated with their sexual abuse. As children they may have subsumed negative connotations of the abuse into part of their self-image. They may see themselves as responsible for the abuse because their badness somehow caused it. Some may believe they were betrayed because they were bad. They may also believe that the secrecy surrounding the abuse somehow made them accomplices in the abuse; this belief reinforces their sense of badness. The goodness perspective addresses these issues within the subthemes of trust, responsibility, and secrecy.

During groups 18 through 22, Angie began to consider the issue of blame. She recalled telling her mother about the incest with her brother. Her mother didn't believe her and the abuse escalated. Angie asked, "Who is to blame—my mother, my brother, or me for not telling someone else?" She further wondered, "Is there something wrong with me that I keep getting abused?" Twyla acknowledged feeling guilt about "keeping the incest a secret" and stated, "The secrecy bonded me to him and forced me to hold onto something that felt bad and shameful." Kate joined the discussion by saying, "My husband doesn't understand why I didn't tell anyone what was happening when I was a kid. I know I wanted it to stop so why didn't I tell?" Dorie admitted to wanting continued secrecy and said, "I would never be able to look people in the eye if they knew about my grandfather and me." Ann related to the discussion of blame and secrecy by exploring trust. She said, "How can you ever trust someone when you know everyone keeps secrets. As I get new memories, I wonder if I can even trust myself." As intermember trust deepened, they began to disclose shameful past behaviors. Ann confessed to "liking her brother's attention" and to "responding physically to his sexual abuse." Twyla confessed to having been physically abusive of her children, and Kate confessed to hating her sexual relationship with her husband. Dorie, who revealed a past affair with a coworker, said, "I've felt so ashamed about it I've never told anyone."

THE SUBTHEME OF TRUST

Incest survivors have significant concerns about trust and betrayal (Finkelhor & Browne, 1985; Bergart, 1986; Brandt, 1989). The betrayal they experienced through the incest may cause them to question people's basic goodness. This is especially likely if the offender was someone they trusted or if they were abused by multiple perpetrators. The feeling of betrayal may extend to mothers, other family members, teachers, or other adults who did not protect them. Members may angrily recall how, during childhood, no adult explored the reasons for their physical and/or emotional symptoms. A few recall telling others about the abuse as a child but were disbelieved or punished. As adults, some continue to believe that people will betray them. Therefore, to protect themselves, they may avoid intimate relationships. However, members who are too trusting of other people may idealize them and excuse their faults. Whether trusting too much or not trusting at all, members may not feel that they deserve respectful relationships in which trust can develop.

Self-trust may also be an issue. Many mistrust their own judgments, emotions, and ability to protect themselves. When self-trust is seen from the perspective of power, it relates to the ability to make choices to protect oneself physically and emotionally. From the goodness perspective, trust relates to a belief in self-goodness. If members believe they are basically good people, they may be more likely to trust themselves.

Therapeutic Goal: Facilitate Trust

Cognitive/Behavioral Issues. Members may be encouraged to define trust and review how to judge the trustworthiness of others.
They may need to realize that no one can be responsive or trustworthy at all times. As trust is discussed, members may be advised to
trust others in steps or stages. During each stage, they may judge
the other people's trustworthiness based on behavior. The group
may also analyze trust by discussing how they, as group members,
have moved through stages of trust.

Self-trust may likewise be addressed. Members may be asked how
they define self-trust or how they know when they can trust themselves. They may also explore self-trust by identifying the "parts of
themselves" that trust others. For example, Angie identified an "adolescent within" who doesn't trust anyone and a "little girl within"
who trusts everyone. Likewise, members may identify "internal
parts" they trust and do not trust. For example, Ann labeled her self-
destructiveness as a "depressed ten-year-old who wants to die." She
realizes that she does not trust this part but does trust an "adult part
who has some hope."

The leader should keep in mind that remarks that may seem trivial
to her or him may seem significant to others. If members' behaviors
indicate shame or anger, they should be asked to clarify their thoughts
and reactions. Such processing will likely enhance the trust level
within the group. Group trust will also be enhanced if the leader be-
haves in a trustworthy manner by following through on any promises,
being on time for group, reassuring members about confidentiality,
and being open about her or his thoughts and reactions. Because members may have been conditioned to expect betrayal, the leader will
be watched carefully for any signs of untrustworthiness.

Emotional Issues. The leader may address emotional issues by
emphasizing and discussing group experiences related to trust. For
example, during one group session, Angie discussed her mother's
unsupportive attitude, asking, "Don't mothers understand that their
kids need to come first some time?" After noticing Twyla's with-
drawal, the leader asked, "Twyla, how are you feeling about what
Angie shared?" Twyla responded, "Angie talked about her mother

right after I talked about my daughter. It's like she was trying to tell me that I'm not a good mother." Angie responded to Twyla by saying, "That is not what I meant. I can tell you really care about your children. You are not like my mother." Twyla was then able to understand how her emotions were influenced by her misperceptions regarding trust. The leader then encouraged all the members to explore their own perceptions and emotional reactions regarding trust or mistrust.

THE SUBTHEME OF RESPONSIBILITY

Self-Blame

Incest survivors often blame themselves for the incest and related problems. Summit (1983) postulates that self-blame is one way victims accommodate the abuse. Self-blame also allows a victim to maintain a positive view of their families. For example, van der Kolk (1987) suggests that an abused child accomplishes this by "splitting the image of the abusive parent into good and bad parts" (p. 134). This process may allow the victim to see only good in their parents and only bad in themselves. They are then able to clarify blame (I am bad and at fault) while remaining loyal to his or her family (they are good and not to blame). Offenders often reinforce this view of blame by verbally or nonverbally blaming the victim (O'Connell, Leberg & Donaldson, 1990). The child victim's tendency to blame herself or himself for the incest often continues into adulthood and extends to a generalized pattern of self-blame (Gold, 1986).

Conversely, a few members may absolve themselves of responsibility for all past behaviors. They do not blame themselves for the abuse but they also do not assess guilt at other times when they should. They may place blame for their hurtful, even abusive behaviors of others on their abusive past (Drews & Bradley, 1989), their poor self-esteem, or their loneliness.

Shame and Guilt

Self-blame about the incest or other past behaviors often results in feelings of shame and guilt. Our experience indicates that members in our groups reveal the most shame and self-blame when discussing two types of past behaviors: negative parenting styles and inappropriate sexual behaviors. Because members have likely discussed the harm resulting from victimization, those who have been abusive of children may be extremely hesitant to disclose that fact. For example, after Twyla acknowledged her past abusive behaviors regarding her own children, she said, "You talk about how your families screwed you up. I feel I've done that to my own children." She went on to describe how she had tried to compensate for her abusive behaviors by being "the best mother a child could want." Such compensating behavior may extend beyond parenting to other relationships and endeavors. Victims may believe that they can make up for their perceived badness by being perfect. Often, however, they embrace such extremely high standards that their efforts never result in the sense of goodness they long for.

Shame about past sexual behavior may stem from the incest, promiscuous sexual behaviors, past affairs, lesbian relationships, and/or sexual fantasies. Some victims recall experiencing physical pleasure as a result of the abuse and now feel intense shame about their responsiveness. Others feel shame about liking the attention they received from their abuser. Because of these reactions, the victims may view themselves as responsible for all aspects of the incestuous relationship even if some incidents were forced or violent. Some may modify their beliefs regarding responsibility but still experience shame regarding sexual feelings. Some believe, "If I feel pleasure related to sex, that means I'm bad." Those who are able to enjoy sexual interactions may feel shame about their choice of sexual partners. Some may have behaved promiscuously, had affairs with married men or with partners significantly younger or older.

Although lesbian members who enter group may be prepared to disclose their sexual preference, some are anxious about doing so because being lesbian is still taboo in our society (Mara, 1983). They may not feel personal shame regarding their preference but are aware of the shaming messages reflected by our society in general. Other members, especially those who have not had close associations with women who are lesbian, may struggle with accepting the lesbian member's preference and lifestyle without feeling personally threatened. Issues related to lesbianism may also cause some members to question and seek clarification of their own sexual identity.

Therapeutic Goal: Clarify Responsibilities

Cognitive/Behavioral Issues. Assigning responsibility regarding the incest itself may be easier if the abuse was violent or forced. This may be more difficult for members, like Ann, who participated or physically responded to the abuse. The leader should clarify that physical responsiveness does not connote complicity (O'Hare & Taylor, 1983). Although Ann may have had limited responsibility for being physically available to her brother, she was encouraged to view her behavior in the context of the family dynamics. The group also helped Ann to understand how her peer-like relationship with her brother (she was six and her brother was eight when the incest began), her emotional isolation from peers, and her father's physical abuse all influenced her need for her brother's affection and support. As the group helped Ann assess her culpability, her mother's role in the family was highlighted. For many members, issues regarding a mother's non-protection may be as distressing as issues related to the offender's behavior (Tsai & Wagner, 1978). By analyzing the offender's and mother's roles, as well as other family of origin dynamics, members may begin to understand how their self-blaming patterns and the accompanying shame developed. Members, like Kate, may experience distress as a result of this clarification process because they feel intense loyalty to the offender and family. Kate was hesitant to assign blame to her father because she feared that then "she would have to hate him." Some members do expect others to develop hatred for the offender. The leader, however, should inform the group that many survivors experience both love and hate regarding the offender and family, and they need not choose between these extreme feelings. Rather, they need to learn how to cope with and accept the mixed feelings.

Discussions of forgiveness of others and of one's self should coincide with the process of clarifying responsibility. Members are encouraged to view forgiveness as a process of acknowledging the past and detaching from it. If they forgive others (let go of emotions and attachments), it does not imply that they condone the incest. Likewise, it does not imply that they should have relationships with others who hurt them. As members clarify responsibility for the incest, they may need to acknowledge that they too are capable of hurting others. If they can acknowledge and accept their negative behavior in a safe context like the group, they may then learn how harmful behavior patterns can be changed. Defining ways to make reparation to those they hurt may be helpful in the self-forgiveness process. Reparation may be direct, such as apologizing to the person, or indirect, such as writing letters which are not sent. Members may also assist each other in the self-forgiveness process by affirming the goodness in one another even though they are aware of their "shameful" past behaviors. As members realize that others can forgive them, they may be able to forgive themselves. As members clarify responsibilities for the incest, past offending behaviors, and past sexual behaviors, they should also assess the accuracy and effects of shame producing beliefs. Beliefs such as, "I was abused because I was bad" or "I made the abuse happen because I wanted attention" may be viewed as assessments made during childhood which are no longer accurate or helpful. Similarly, beliefs regarding their own abusive behaviors can be assessed. For example, after Twyla discussed hurting her children she concluded, "I am just as bad as my father." Through feedback from other members, Twyla realized that although she hurt her child, she acknowledged her abusive behavior and made reparation to her daughter. Because her father never acknowledged his abusive behavior or made any reparation, she could conclude, "I may hurt others at times, but I'm not like my father."

General discussions of sexuality are often intregal to the process of clarifying responsibility. The first step is often education. Members should be given information about the differences between affectionate touch and sexual touch, common arousal patterns for men and women, the influence of stress on sexual responsiveness, common sexual dysfunctions, and normal sexual behaviors. As these topics are discussed, members should be encouraged to reformulate beliefs about sexual behavior. Beliefs such as, "I am dirty if I enjoy sex" may change to "As an adult, I am free to enjoy my body's sensations." Books which refer to incest and sexuality such as Maltz and Holman's *Incest and Sexuality* (1987) and Jehu's *Beyond Sexual Abuse: Therapy with Women who were Childhood Victims* (1988) may be helpful for some members.

When the topic of sexual preference is introduced, the leader may choose to review Maltz and Holman's (1987) distinction between lesbians who happen to be incest survivors and those who choose lesbian relationships because of the incest. The discussion of lesbian lifestyles may be especially difficult for women who were sexually abused by a female perpetrator (Abney et al., 1992). The leader should pay particular attention to these members so they have the opportunity to express their views and feelings.

Emotional Issues. A review of concepts related to shame and guilt may assist members in resolving shame and guilt. Shame may be defined as an "ongoing premise that one is fundamentally bad, inadequate, defective, unworthy, or not fully valid as a human being" (Fossum & Mason, 1986, p. 5). Shame is accompanied by emotions such as embarrassment, mortification, and humiliation. Guilt may be defined as actions prohibited by social custom (Fisher, 1985). It may be helpful to have members associate guilt with behavior and shame with emotions. After clarifying these concepts, members may realize that experiencing shame (emotion) does not necessarily imply guilt (wrongful action). They may then be able to more rationally evaluate past actions by assessing and accepting varying degrees of their responsibility.

THE SUBTHEME OF SECRECY

The secrecy surrounding the abuse often intensifies the victim's shame (Summit, 1983). As children, victims may not have been aware that the abuse was wrong until they were told to keep the activity secret. In addition to shame, they may have experienced a sense of power because they were keeping a secret that could destroy their family (Meiselman, 1990). Whether it produced shame, power, or both, the secrecy often promoted a special bond between the victim and offender. The child may therefore have felt isolated because the secrecy formed a barrier to relationships with other family members. Unfortunately, isolation may have been reinforced even when the secrecy was broken. Some members report that they were called a liar, blamed as causing the abuse, or punished for telling. Some members who did not disclose the incest until adulthood also report negative results. A few members report that spouses or friends accused them, subtly or directly, of being compliant to the abuse because they kept it a secret. A few do not disclose the incest until they enter therapy.

The theme of secrecy may also refer to people's potential to conceal badness. Many victims fear that if the offender had "secret badness," then perhaps anyone could. Secrecy may also be used to describe "hidden parts of self." Ann felt, as new memories emerged, that there were hidden secrets within her. Dorie, who experienced psychosomatic symptoms, often asked, "What is my body trying to tell me?" Viewing these symptoms from the perspective of goodness and secrecy may allow members to understand and cope with these symptoms in a new way. Although members fear being unable to recognize their's and others' secrets, some report feeling like their secrets are transparent to others. It is as if the word "incest" is written on their foreheads. Thus, their shameful past is exposed for all to see.

Therapeutic Goal: Encourage Openness

Cognitive/Behavioral Issues. The very act of attending an incest therapy group breaks secrecy about the incest. Therefore, secrets, instead of forming a barrier, can become a unifying force in the group (Laube & Wieland, 1990). The leader may encourage members to explore secrecy as being both helpful and/or destructive. Members may learn that as adults, they have choices about what they share of themselves. At times, they may keep secrets from others not because the secrets are shameful, but because they choose not to share them. Conversely, disclosing secrets may affirm their sense of internal goodness. Bergart (1986) describes the group as being like a "hall of mirrors" (p. 270) in which members see themselves in others. As members accept one another as good people, even though others have "bad" secrets, they may be closer to accepting themselves as good people despite their own secret "badness." Members, through feedback and self-acceptance, may further realize that they are not transparent to others.

Emotional Issues. Self-secrecy may also be described in positive or negative terms. Describing psychological defenses as a form of self-secrecy may help members understand the purpose of their defensive structure and give them ideas about how to modify it. For example, members may be encouraged to view emotional defenses as "internal helping walls that keep memories hidden" until the person is strong enough to cope with them. Likewise, members who are like Dorie can be in- structed to view their physical symptoms as "their bodies' way of telling them" that some emotions need to be acknowledged and released. Defenses may also be described as coping mechanisms that have, for the most part, outlived their useful- ness. Members, rather than feeling bad for having strong defenses, may learn to view themselves as having been resourceful and creative in the ways they learned to cope with the incest and the secrets as children.

❏ The Importance Perspective

The importance perspective relates to a survivor's sense of worth. Many women in our groups recall feeling as if they were treated like objects, not human beings, during the incest experience. Offenders' needs were clearly more important than their own. As a result, these women may have learned to disregard themselves as worthwhile human beings. In addition to low self-worth, members describe con- fusion about the incest experience itself. As children they were well aware that the incest had occurred, but their family often acted as if it had not. Because of the offender's and the family's denial, the child's reality was often negated, which left her or him to wonder what was real and what was not (Courtois, 1988). Even as adults, members may question the importance and validity of the incest experience.

The importance perspective addresses these issues by exploring emotional connections, personal significance, and identity. The con- nection subtheme addresses questions such as "Am I important enough to belong to a group?"; "Am I important enough to be validated by my family"; or "Am I important enough to be respected by others?" The significance subtheme refers to issues of self-esteem and personal purpose, while the identity subtheme explores survi- vors' self-conceptions.

During groups 20 through 24, members began to analyze their role(s) and function regarding group and other relationships. Twyla, for the first time, did not go to her parent's home for the holidays, but instead spent time with her daughters. This behavior was her declaration that "the incest is a part of my past and I don't need to pretend anymore." Dorie began to sort out how the incest fits into her present life by exploring its meaning. This process led her to reassess her opinions regarding herself and others. She wondered, "If I was wrong in my assessment about the incest, may I have been wrong in my self-assessments? I used to think I was a cold and rigid person. Now I'm beginning to realize those are my mother's words—not mine." Likewise, Angie began to explore "what she wanted to do with the rest of her life." She declared, "It's time to put all this family junk behind me." Kate, with others' strong encouragement, began to consider limiting her Sunday family gatherings. She admitted to desperately needing her family, but described how family and other relationships "wear her out." Kate began one group by saying, "Before therapy I thought I knew who I was and what I was supposed to do. Now it seems I don't know either." Ann, who had maintained emotional distance from her family, considered confronting her brother so she could have a more open relationship with her entire family. Also, she began to feel less depressed and more hopeful about her future.

THE SUBTHEME OF CONNECTION

Childhood incest may affect an individual's ability to engage in satisfying adult interpersonal relationships (see Chapter 1). The range of survivors' social functioning may vary from isolation to extreme emotional dependency. Some who are extremely dependent may so fear abandonment that any emotional attachment, even with abusive people, may be preferable to being alone. They, like Kate, may maintain relationships by pleasing others. Their personal needs are therefore secondary to the need for interpersonal connection. Some become so emotionally involved in others' lives that they "lose themselves." These patterns associated with emotional dependency may be described as "codependent" (Schaef, 1986). This term is commonly used to label clients with relationship concerns and should, as Briere (1992) cautions, be used carefully with abuse survivors. What may be labeled as "codependent" behavior may have been adaptive behavior that was learned in the abusive context (Briere, 1992). Functioning at the other extreme are members who may be called "antidependent." Although frightened of being alone, they are even more frightened of emotional intimacy. They believe that any emotionally close relationship will eventually become hurtful. To avoid that inevitable pain, they maintain emotionally distant relationships and make connections with others only around tasks such as work or sports. Or, they may not connect at all.

For many members, relationships with family of origin are most problematic. Recent research indicates that negative family experiences, such as emotional and physical abuse, may be as damaging as the sexual abuse itself (Edwards & Alexander, 1992; Harter et al., 1988). Therefore, working with family of origin issues should be a central focus of incest therapy groups. Although it may be possible for members to maintain good relationships with some or all members of their family, members still report various problems and desires in regard to their families. Some want a relationship with their family, but feel that the incest is a barrier to present day interactions with them. They, like Ann, may want to discuss the abuse so they can "be themselves" when they're with their family. Unfortunately, for some, when they confront their families, the past abuse is minimized or denied. They may then need to determine the extent to which they can maintain any family connections. Some want to confront their families so they can sever ties with them. Others choose not to confront, but maintain a cordial but distant relationship with their families. A few, like Kate, desire a closer relationship with their families and are willing to go along with denial of the abuse so the "close" relationship can exist.

Family of origin difficulties may be especially troublesome during holidays. Special family days such as Christmas, Easter, Mother's Day or Father's Day may trigger unresolved issues. Some members, who attend holiday festivities and act as if the incest isn't problematic, feel as if they are betraying themselves. Others, who choose not to attend family gatherings, may feel guilty.

Therapeutic Goal: Support Healthy Relationships

Cognitive/Behavioral Issues. It is helpful to provide education about interpersonal boundaries. Members can be informed that boundaries, both physical and emotional, should be distant enough to allow for self-protection but open enough to allow for meaningful interpersonal connections. Members who tend to function with extreme dependency may be encouraged to distance themselves from certain relationships. The group may assist them by suggesting or exploring possible distancing strategies. Those who function at the "antidependent" extreme may be encouraged to begin to foster more emotional closeness.

The decision of whether or not to confront the family about the abuse is an important boundary issue. Although a momentum for confrontation may sweep the group, members should be cautioned that confrontation may be either helpful or damaging. MacFarlane and Korbin (1983) suggest that members who confront should be prepared for denial, delayed reactions, family crisis, or a lack of validation or apology. Regardless of the type of response they receive, many may feel more power and confidence because of the confrontation (Cole, 1985). Each member should assess her motivation for confronting, what results she would expect, and what risks and benefits would be involved. This decision maybe complicated by the fact that the offender may now behave differently than he or she did when the abuse occurred. Kate, confused by this, would state that her father was now a "gentle and supportive man"—much different from the man who sexually abused her.

The group can offer much support and encouragement for those who choose to confront. Members may write out their confrontation and share it with the group for feedback. They may also rehearse the confrontation with other group members who role-play the family. At times, group members may even accompany the confronting member to the family meeting. Those who choose not to confront may work with symbolic confrontations (Siegel & Romig, 1988; Apolinsky & Wilcoxin, 1991) through role plays or imagery. A few may choose a legal confrontation and sue their offender (Moore, 1986).

Some groups, in addressing family of origin issues, choose to undertake an in-depth analysis by taking time out for a "family of origin project." During this project, members may conduct history gathering interviews with family members and outline the family tree which is presented to the group for analysis. If group trust is high, members may role-play a common family scene (such as mealtime). During the role play, members play themselves and choose other group members to role play their family members. Acting out these types of role plays have been a powerful way for members to experience and understand their place in their family.

After exploring various family of origin issues, members may be able to define the kind of current relationship they prefer to have with their family. Some may need to create more physical distance with parents while others may need to practice maintaining clear emotional boundaries. Members, like Kate, may have difficulty even conceiving plans to have a more distant relationship with parents and siblings. Other group members may assist them in outlining small steps that could facilitate more distance. Through the process of exploring desired roles, members may finally give themselves permission to make their own needs a priority.

Emotional Issues. Although liberating, enacting healthy boundaries may precipitate further grieving for "the family that will never be." As relationships with family of origin are redefined, members may begin to focus on their families of procreation and other intimate relationships. For some members, the relationship with the group becomes a primary focus. Group may provide them the only setting where they can be open about their past and be fully accepted. The group, who then emotionally replaces their family of origin, may feel like a new family.

THE SUBTHEME OF SIGNIFICANCE

Incest survivors often report feelings of insignificance (see Chapter 1). Some resist being recognized as important because they fear rejection or even abuse. They reason, "If I am significant then I will be noticed and this may lead to further abuse." To protect themselves from being important to others, they may dismiss others' positive affirmations as lacking in authenticity. Others may want recognition but believe they need to be transformed before they can be important. They may reason, "If I am not significant for who I am, then maybe I should be someone else." They may idolize others and attempt to be like them—hoping that by acting like someone else, they can be seen as important. A few may believe, "No one will notice me unless I make them notice." These members often make themselves the center of attention and may behave in grandiose or aggressive ways. Unfortunately, such behavior tends to isolate them.

Some members feel unable to assess themselves as worthy and significant because the incest and/or family environment seems to disprove their worth. To incorporate the incest experience and still feel self-worth, they may need to find meaning in the experience. Silver, Boon, and Stones (1983) report that over 80% of the incest survivors in their group continued to search for a meaning, reason, or a way to make sense of the incest experience. They also found that those who defined the incest as meaningful in some way experienced less psychological distress, better social adjustment, higher levels of self-esteem and greater resolution to the experience. However, the searching process may also trigger disturbing memories and psychological distress especially if the search continues for an extended period of time.

Therapeutic Goal: Illustrate Significance

Cognitive/Behavioral Issues. Members may be encouraged to explore questions such as: "What is meaningful in my life now?"; "How am I significant to others?"; and "How can I contribute to the world in a meaningful way?" Because some members may be unable to acknowledge their own importance, it may be helpful for members to answer these questions for each other. They may also benefit from practicing self-talk which asserts their importance or by verbally asserting their importance in front of the group. For example, Ann was asked to say to the group, "I am important to others." Discussion of self-caring behaviors may also help them in asserting their importance. Members may be encouraged, at times, to put their needs ahead of others. The group may brainstorm about nurturing things they can do for themselves. Suggestions may include: finding a safe place where they can practice relaxation or take time-outs, buying themselves gifts, and/or surrounding themselves with caring people. With such encouragements, the group can serve as "cheerleaders" who reinforce and applaud self-caring behaviors.

To facilitate the assignment of meaning, the leader may ask: "Why do you believe you were abused?"; "How is the incest meaningful to you now?"; or "How can something good come from something so bad?" As members answer these questions, it is beneficial for them to ventilate feelings, talk about the incest experience, and learn about the dynamics which accompany incest (Silver, Boon, and Stones, 1983). Most members make sense of the abuse by attributing responsibility to their dysfunctional families or to an emotionally disturbed offender. A few may conclude that the incest made them sensitive to others, allowed them to develop strength, or promoted their spiritual development.

A discussion of meaning and importance often leads to discussion of spiritual concerns. Religious/spiritual concerns may be especially relevant for those who have been abused by a member of the clergy or by offenders who professed to being "religious." Although the therapist should avoid advocating any religious orientation (Meiselman, 1990), she or he can encourage discussion about beliefs and emotions related to spirituality. Some members, who recall how they prayed for the abuse to stop, may discuss their anger and disappointment with God. Others may discuss their difficulty with patriarchal religious structures (Courtois, 1988). Such discussions should allow members to formulate new ideas about spirituality that are more applicable to their present life. Members who want to explore spiritual issues in depth are often referred for formal spiritual counseling.

Emotional Issues. The group process may be explored to assist members in experiencing their importance. Recognizing members' roles and purpose within the group may allow them to experience how they are important to each other. Members may be asked to validate how each member plays an important and unique role in the group. Members who experience themselves as peripheral to the group process may focus on how they could feel more important within the group.

THE SUBTHEME OF IDENTITY

Identity is categorized within the importance perspective because it is assumed that survivors will not define themselves as important until they have a consistent and positive identity. Survivors of severe maltreatment may experience an impaired self-reference (Briere, 1992). They may have difficulty viewing themselves in a consistent manner and, therefore, may have no reliable base from which to interact with others. As a result, they may display attachment difficulties and dysfunctional self-perceptions. These patterns may have originated as a way to cope with the abuse. Because their perceptions and reactions to the abuse did not match what they were told or had observed, they invalidated their own reactions. For example, Angie recalled being told by her father that his touching was a way to show how much he cared about her, but she remembered feeling degraded and frightened. Because these viewpoints were discrepant, she had to choose which viewpoint to adopt. Many choose others' viewpoints to define who they are and what is real. Others choose to depend on their emotional experience for making judgments. Through "emotional reasoning" (Jehu, 1988), survivors use their emotions to judge their perceptions. For example, they may judge someone to be angry only because they feel threatened or angry themselves. Likewise, if they experience fear in someone's presence, they may believe the other person is dangerous.

Some profess to have a stable, but negative self-concept. They believe they are bad and this badness forms the foundation of their identity. They may fear that if the negative beliefs and accompanying self-hatred were to change, they would crumble. These members often reject others' positive assessments of them as misguided or uninformed. It is common to hear statements like, "If you only knew what I was really like, you wouldn't like me." They also defend their negative self-concept by recounting their many transgressions. Some even label themselves as being as bad as the offender.

Therapeutic Goal: Clarify a Positive Identity

Cognitive/Behavioral Issues. To work toward developing a positive identity, members may be introduced to basic cognitive exercises such as analyzing their self-talk, clarifying basic beliefs, and identifying irrational beliefs. Members may be asked to formulate an identity list (Drews & Bradley, 1989) through which they complete the statement, "I am . . ." regarding various issues such as power, responsibility, goodness. To assist in judging people or situations, members may be encouraged to assess objective information (such as behavior) separate from what others tell them. Feedback from other members can help them see people or situations from new and helpful perspectives. The leader should encourage members to discover a balance between trusting their own feelings and basing judgments on objective data.

Cognitive approaches may be especially helpful when analyzing the offender's behavior. Members may begin to understand the reasons for the offender's viewpoints (he said those things so he could rationalize the abuse). They may also understand how they incorporated his or her viewpoints (I believed him because he was more powerful). Members may then be able to discern how their current beliefs reflect the offender's viewpoints and decide whether such beliefs are applicable or helpful to them as adults.

Emotional Issues. The leader may assist members in their identity explorations by introducing ideas such as ego or emotional states of mind, parts of self, or the "child/adolescent within." In applying these concepts, members are asked to "embody" a pattern of thought or emotion into an image of a child/adolescent. For example, when Ann talked about an incident that occurred when she was six, the leader asked her, "What did that six-year-old feel?" Ann replied, "Scared and hopeless." Subsequently, when Ann experienced that feeling state (scared and hopeless), she was encouraged to envision it as the six-year-old. After guiding an individual member in such a process, the leader should include the group by asking about everyone's own "scared little girls." It then may be helpful for them to visualize themselves as an adult comforting that scared child. If this is difficult, members may assist each other to envision this or they may imagine how they as a group would have protected and comforted all the scared children. The leader may also guide the entire group to imagine themselves as children or adolescents, and then have them share how they would be interacting in the group at that particular age. Or, members may imagine themselves as adults "bringing" their little girl/adolescent to group and talking for her. Processes such as these often help members to discover how little girl or adolescent beliefs and emotions still influence them as adults. They may also understand how their "adult selves" versus their "little girl/adolescent selves" think, feel, and behave. Members may also be assisted in understanding these "parts" by reviewing information regarding child development. As they understand parts of themselves, they may begin to accept parts that have been separated from their core identity. They may realize, for example, that the vulnerable little girl who was victimized and contaminated is still "alive." As they join with her rather than ostracize her, they may experience a renewed sense of wholeness and worth. If members have difficulty with envisioning children within, they may use other metaphors, such as a volcano or dark pit, to assist them in containing the feeling or ego states (Groves & Panzer, 1989).

❏ Summary

The group therapist may use the Power, Goodness and Importance (PGI) framework to analyze group discussions from a perspective which relates to incest. Some group topics, such as secrecy, clearly indicate the most applicable perspective and subtheme. Other topics, such as problems with a coworker, may be viewed from any of the PGI perspectives. In those situations, the therapist may present all the perspectives or simply choose one. The following example serves to illustrate the process of applying the PGI framework.

It was the fifteenth session and all members were present. Angie had opened the discussion by describing a recent date "with another loser." There was a silence after which Ann began to cry saying, "What is the use of trying anyway? Nothing good ever seems to happen." Other members remained silent and looked to the leader for direction. The leader's thoughts were:

> It's too soon for me to comment. I'm not sure which perspective would be most helpful. I will look to Ann, awaiting further comment.

The group, taking their cue from the leader, looked back to Ann. Ann remained silent and Twyla finally commented, "I know just how you feel. Sometimes it is hard to keep going." The leader, staying with her plan to monitor, remained silent. Kate then spoke, "Sometimes I get scared when Ann is depressed. I keep remembering the time she talked about killing herself. I wish I could say something to make it better." After Kate's comment the therapist thought:

> It seems that the Perspective of Power may be helpful especially regarding hopelessness. Because Kate is talking about feeling helpless, I will intervene with her instead of naming the perspective to the group.

The leader said, "Kate, I'm hearing that you feel helpless regarding what to tell Ann. I'm interested in how you handle those feelings when they come to you." Kate then talked a bit about how she "tries to look on the bright side of things" which prompted Angie to say, "Get real! You can't do that all the time. What's it like when your dad comes and watches you all day." Kate immediately began to cry and the leader thought:

> This is not what I had hoped for. Now Angie has confronted Kate and I would bet she feels attacked. The Power Perspective still seems helpful, but more from the vantage point of safety. I'd better mediate a process intervention and try to illustrate how the group can provide both a sense of hope as well as safety. I'll start with Kate.

The leader directed a comment to Kate, "Kate, how are you feeling toward Angie right now?" Kate, after crying for a bit longer, said something which surprised everyone, "I am sick and tired of her always trying to make everyone feel bad." Angie, needing no prompting, responded, "I'm sorry, I didn't mean to hurt you. But I'm glad I made you mad. That's the first time I've ever heard you stand up for yourself." The leader's thoughts were:

> I like the way Angie responded. She is reinforcing Kate for asserting some power. I'll just let them go on for a bit.

Kate then responded, "You know it felt kind of good, but I hope I didn't hurt your feelings, Angie." After a pause the therapist said, "Angie, can you respond to Kate's concern?" Angie said, "No, I'm not mad, I had it coming. I just wish I could be gentler sometimes. I'm afraid I scare people." The leader's thoughts then were:

> Perfect. Now Angie has opened it up to the theme of safety within the group. Now I can mediate a process discussion about group safety.

The leader then asked the remaining members to respond to Angie's concern as well as share other issues regarding group safety. Although some acknowledged feeling unsafe in the group, they all agreed that "Angie means well." The leader thought:

> Now that the group feels more interactive and open, I'll go back to Ann's comments and encourage some discussion of hope especially as it relates to the group. I may enact a messenger function to let them know that hope is essential for recovery.

The leader then commented, "I'd like to get back to what Ann talked about earlier. It seems you are feeling hopeless about many things but yet feel powerless to change them. I'm hoping the group feels safe enough so you can explore your hopelessness." The group then discussed the topic of hope and seemed more hopeful when they left.

As this example indicates, the therapist needs to maintain an internal assessment process through which interventions are planned. The PGI framework can assist in this process as the therapist asks, "How can the power, goodness and importance perspectives be applied?"

4

The Active Ongoing
Therapy Group

This chapter highlights the functions of the therapist by describing the development of a typical group from beginning to intermediate to more advanced phases. As each phase is described, the monitor, mediator, messenger, and member functions (4 Ms) are clarified. We continue to use the group introduced in chapter 3, but rather than concentrating on the content themes, we now focus on the therapist's assessments and interventions regarding process issues in the group.

❏ The First Group Session

The first group therapy session sets the stage for all that follows. In pregroup training, the therapist takes an active messenger role and clients act more as passive recipients. In therapy group, the therapist, through monitoring and mediating, challenges members to expand their roles from passive recipients to active helpers. Because interactional patterns that occur during the first meeting often become long term, these role changes must be reinforced from the very beginning. Members who do not learn to be involved with each other during the first meeting will likely remain uninvolved throughout subsequent sessions.

Opening comments not only begin the first meeting, they also set the tone for subsequent sessions. The leader should begin the group with an opening statement that changes the tone from pregroup to therapy group; invites (not demands) all members to respond; and reflects the tone of feelings in the room. Examples of opening statements are: "We've been preparing to start therapy for the last few weeks and I'm a little anxious. I'm sensing others might be feeling anxious as well. Am I reading that right?"; "The feeling in the room seems a little tense. What is it like being here now that therapy is beginning?"; or "As I look around I guess that people are experiencing a mixture of feelings about starting therapy. Can you share what you are feeling right now?" After members have responded to the leader's opening comments, the leader invites them to set the direction for the remainder of the meeting by saying, "As we discussed during pregroup training, this is the time for you to begin to take over. You may share whatever issues seem important to you." By saying this, the therapist reminds members that they have the responsibility to introduce topics for discussion.

> Only Twyla, Kate, and Ann responded verbally to the opening question by sharing their anxiety about therapy; Angie and Dorie nodded in agreement. Ann then began to cry and discussed a past group experience that was hurtful, indeed harmful, to her. There was silence, after which Kate talked about her father's frequent visits to her home. She related feeling guilty for being in group, saying, "It's like I'm doing something bad to him." Twyla immediately responded by discussing her hatred for her own father. She stated emphatically, "I wouldn't let that lowlife near my house!" She then went on to share information about a past dating relationship in which she was physically and sexually abused. After a long pause Dorie expressed her pessimism about the group process—especially in light of Ann's comments. Angie shared little beyond her name.

THERAPIST AS MONITOR AND MEDIATOR
DURING THE FIRST SESSION

Despite the pregroup training, members may begin the therapy process feeling unsafe. Some, like Ann, may have negative feelings about both the leader and the group, while some, like Dorie, may be skeptical about therapy in general. The monitoring function itself may be threatening. Because members may have been aware of being watched by their perpetrator(s), the leader's observing behavior may trigger some uncomfortable responses. Members may wonder, "What is the leader really thinking about me?"; "What does this leader have up her sleeve?"; or "How will she hurt me?"

Although the most productive group format is unstructured and freely interacting (Yalom, 1985), some members may feel safer if there is a structure for dividing group time. The leader, therefore, should guide the group in a time management structure that promotes free interaction similar to what would occur in normal relationships. Many groups decide to structure a "check-in time" at the beginning of each group, much the same as one would update a friend. During check-in, members share the week's events and indicate their need for group time and attention. We advise that check-in be brief. Otherwise some members may "check-in" for most of the group's time. Some groups decide on a more informal beginning during which members simply indicate whether or not they need time to discuss an issue.

Some members, like Twyla, share very personal information during the first meeting, while others, like Angie, choose to share little or nothing. When members disclose too much before trust is developed, they may end up feeling terrified because of the risks they took and get angry at the group and the leader for allowing the risk (O'Hare & Taylor, 1983). Conversely, members who remain silent may experience guilt about not contributing to the group. The leader should determine the balance between sharing too much and too little and discourage or encourage members to disclose accordingly. For example, Twyla could have been discouraged from too much disclosure if the leader had commented, "You are sharing very personal information with women you don't know well, and I am concerned about how you might feel later. Could you stop for a bit and discuss how you feel about revealing what you have?" Likewise, a member like Angie, who had been silent for a period of time, could have been invited to participate in a noninvasive way if the leader said, "I've noticed you have been quiet so far. Would you feel comfortable sharing how the meeting is going for you?"

These quotes are examples of a central mediating process called process focus (Yalom, 1985). The comments used in the above example encouraged Twyla and Angie to reflect on their behavior in the group rather than focusing on the content of what they were saying. In addition to focusing on an individual's behavior, the leader may focus on the group as a whole by initiating a process discussion from one of the power, goodness, and importance (PGI) perspectives. The leader could have highlighted safety by asking members, "How safe do you feel in the group at this moment?"

Regardless of the type of process focus, it is essential that the leader encourage some process discussion during the first meeting. If this does not occur, the therapist may set a norm implying that the group is really a topic-centered, problem-solving group rather than one that analyzes and discusses its own interactions.

During the first session, members will likely look for direction from the leader. The leader should respond with redirection by inviting members to decide which topics to discuss at their own comfort level. Inexperienced leaders may feel compelled to decrease group tension by choosing topics for the group. However, to facilitate member involvement, the leader should refrain from introducing topics. Because some members will share information more readily than others, the "success" of the first meeting should be measured not by the depth of information shared, but by how issues were related and received.

The closing portion of the first meeting, like the opening, should be planned. Some groups decide on a formal closure, at which time each member reviews the importance of the meeting for herself. Members might also review aspects of the PGI perspectives that were applicable to the group's content. Some groups decide to end on a positive note by either mentioning a positive event about each member's past week or stating something hopeful about the coming week. Whatever form the closing may take, the leader may suggest that it is often helpful for members to leave each meeting with unanswered questions about the issues discussed so they can begin to formulate their own answers.

THERAPIST AS MESSENGER
DURING THE FIRST SESSION

Modeling is a powerful way to teach members about different ways of behaving. In general, the leader should model the positive aspects of power, goodness, and importance by her or his verbal and nonverbal behavior. The leader's behavior should exemplify gentleness, sincerity, confidence, and firmness. The leader's comfort with this role and willingness to share the helper role should be apparent. By refraining from directing the topics, the leader encourages members to make choices about how to help themselves and others. Because the leader treats each group member with respect during this meeting, members may gain a sense of their personal importance to the group.

In addition to modeling, didactic discussions may also be beneficial. A brief discussion about role changes may be helpful if members continue to look to the therapist for direction, but no lecture or topical discussion should be routinely planned for the first meeting. The necessary information regarding the group process should have been given during pregroup training.

THERAPIST AS MEMBER
DURING THE FIRST SESSION

Whether the leader is an experienced therapist or not, she or he may feel insecure and anxious during the first group meeting. It may be helpful for the leader to anticipate her or his reactions before entering the room and to rehearse an opening statement. During pregroup training, the leader may have formed impressions of group members and found that she or he liked some and not others. It is important to monitor those feelings closely so they do not become divisive to the group. Discussing these reactions with a support network is especially helpful.

❑ The Early Phase of Group

During the early phase, the leader's primary task is to facilitate the formation of a group in which members experience a trusting, emotional connection with one another and the group as a whole. This trusting connection, through which the group becomes important to its members, can be termed "cohesion." Cohesion has been described as critical for the developing group (Budman et. al, 1989). One way to help members understand the importance of cohesion may be to describe the group, metaphorically, as a physical body. The power and integrity of the body (group) as a whole depends on each member's care and commitment to it (Laube & Wieland, 1990).

We generally refer to the early stage, when cohesion begins to develop, as lasting from two to nine sessions. The dynamics of the early stage, however, may last much longer, because trust development may vary from a few to many months. Members need to realize that they have time to develop trust, and the therapist must be patient enough to allow for a deep level of trust to develop so members can safely connect with one another.

> Sessions 2 through 9: Throughout the early phase, members attempted to develop trusting relationships with one another. Twyla frequently discussed her struggle with her boss and Ann reported work difficulties that she attributed to her worsening depression. Kate contributed little about her own struggles but gave excellent feedback to others. Kate, Twyla, and Ann were actively involved, while Dorie and Angie seemed peripheral. After about six meetings, a crisis occurred. Angie had been having flashbacks and was frightened about her urge to drink. She phoned Twyla between groups. Twyla, because of a conflict with her daughter, talked with Angie for only a brief time. Angie subsequently drank and skipped the following two groups. When she returned, recommitted to her sobriety, there was a great deal of group discussion about the crisis. Twyla felt guilty and angry; Ann was absorbed with her own addictive struggles; Kate attempted to take care of everyone else; and Dorie seemed especially lost. The leader, who was trying to focus on the struggle while maintaining cohesiveness, was perceived as ineffective (as reported by some of the members' individual therapists) by everyone but Kate. No one, however, confronted the leader directly.

THERAPIST AS MONITOR AND MEDIATOR
IN THE EARLY PHASE

Members may experience an exacerbation of symptoms during the early phase (Donaldson & Edwards, 1988). It is not unusual for members to report "new" memories about abusive experiences, as well as more depression and anxiety. As a result, the victim who is now feeling worse than she was prior to group may wonder, "How is this group helping?" The therapist needs to be verbally reassuring and optimistic in response to such statements by saying, "It is not unusual to feel worse at this stage." Statements like this communicate to members that the therapist believes in the healing process. If the leader has confidence, members will likely begin to feel more confident and hopeful. Occasionally it may become apparent that group is inappropriate, even potentially harmful, for a particular member. That member may be advised to leave the group.

As members form relationships with one another, a small group of members may become friends. These friendships, which are subgroups, occur naturally in most groups (Yalom, 1985). To analyze the presence of potential subgroups, the leader should observe the way members sit within the group, whether or not they stay and talk

Subgroup information should not be kept secret from the group as a whole.

after group, who goes to coffee, and/or who rides to group together. In most cases, the leader need neither encourage nor discourage the development of such friendships. If the leader encourages the exchange of phone numbers or meetings outside of the group sessions, some members may feel forced to develop individual friendships within the group before they are ready. If friendships do develop, the leader should remind members about the rule of no secrets. As a rule, subgroup information should not be kept secret from the group as a whole. Each member needs to make a commitment to abide by this rule before outside friendships begin.

Although subgroups are natural and may provide certain members an opportunity for emotional intimacy, they may also become divisive. For example, the conflict between Angie and Twyla may have been disastrous for the group. To preserve the integrity of the group as a whole, the leader encouraged open discussions of this conflict by asking, "Angie, will you be able to trust Twyla in the group?" and "Twyla, what reactions are you having to Angie, especially considering her relapse?" The leader invited other members into the discussion by asking, "How has it been for you to observe this struggle between Angie and Twyla?" As members discussed their reactions, the leader reinforced Twyla for bringing the conflict to the group and complimented members for their willingness to work on their relationships with one another.

A subgroup that can be most troublesome is a leader/member subgroup. At times, members may stop the leader after group, call between sessions, or schedule individual sessions to discuss personal issues not discussed in the group. These members may strive to have a special or unique relationship with the leader. Maintenance of leader boundaries is especially challenging when members vie for the leader's attention in this way. As with member subgroups, the rule is no secrets. Whatever a member shares with the leader is potentially group information, and the member should be reminded of this rule before any private discussion occurs. It may be particularly difficult for the leader to abide by the no secrets rule when a member or members disclose their dislike for another member. Members who share their negative feelings about another must be asked to discuss their comments with the entire group.

The leader/member subgroup is especially problematic if the group leader is also the individual therapist to any of the members. It is best if the group leader does not function as a member's individual therapist. If this is not possible, boundaries need to be explicitly clarified. The client who is also a group member needs to understand that the leader cannot have a special relationship with her and that pertinent information shared in individual sessions should also be shared in group.

In any case, group therapy needs to be viewed as an integral component of the recovery process. During individual sessions, members may explore various personal issues as well as the meaning of some of the group's dynamics. Members also may rehearse how they will share important information with the group. We usually recommend individual sessions every 4 to 6 weeks (especially during the early phase of group) so that members are able to maintain a relationship with their individual therapist. If the group therapist judges members' symptoms to be too distressful or long lasting, she or he may recommend more frequent individual sessions. When the member's individual therapist is not a member of our therapy team, the group therapist maintains a close working relationship with the individual therapist so both are working toward the same goals.

Intermember comparisons, like subgrouping, may be both positive and negative. On the positive side, members are helped when they can compare their reactions to other incest victims (Herman & Schatzow, 1984). They may seek answers to questions such as "Do you sleep with the light on?"; "Do you still have flashbacks?"; or "Are you afraid of people?" Answers to these kinds of questions can illustrate the members' commonalities so that experiences can become depathologized and normalized (Gilligan & Kennedy, 1989). Members can also begin to experience a feeling of connection to a group of people like themselves.

On the negative side, comparisons can become divisive. Some may believe themselves to be either "sicker" than others or "not bad enough to belong in the group." Others may view themselves as being too emotional, too restrained, smarter than others, or too stupid to belong. These kinds of comparisons are inevitable and indicate each member's struggle to belong and find a role and purpose in the group. They may also reflect transference issues such as rivalry for the leader's attention or unresolved sibling issues (Abney et al., 1992). When the leader observes members' comparisons, she or he can mediate by encouraging open processing: "There seems to be some comparing going on. Can we talk about that for a bit?" The leader may also encourage members to understand the origin of such comparisons by making references to members' families of origin. For example, the leader may comment, "You keep comparing yourself to Kate. Does that fit at all with your reactions to your sister?" or "Is that the way you see your relationship with your father?"

Silences may be problematic in the early phase, especially when members share "shameful" information and others do not respond. The member who shared may then mistakenly believe that others are apathetic or rejecting. In actuality, some of the members listening may have become absorbed in their own memories or emotions. Others may be silent to distance themselves from what is being discussed. The leader may bring the silence to the attention of the group by commenting, "You seem like you are in another world" or "You all seem like you're miles away." The leader then allows the group members to discuss the meaning of their nonresponsiveness. Some members need to be taught about giving verbal feedback even if they become self-absorbed. The therapist may facilitate member feedback by commenting, "How can your identification with Kate's sadness help her resolve it?" or "How can you get beyond your denial to help Ann?" Setting one's own feelings aside to help another may be a new concept for some, and a skill that many need to learn.

The therapist must also monitor how members receive support. For many, receiving support is more challenging than giving support, and the leader should encourage members to accept support openly without needing to discount it. Some members may need to practice saying "thank you." To be able to receive support, members may need to change beliefs such as "I am not good enough to deserve support" or "I am not important enough to receive support."

In the early phase, members often minimize the meaning of tardiness or absences. However, such behavior can be quite detrimental to the group as a whole. It is essential that the therapist intervene about such behaviors with comments such as "I was concerned about your lateness. Is everything O.K.?" or "How did you think Dorie's lateness affected the group today?" Simply recognizing the tardiness may curb such future behavior. If members skip group (absence not prearranged or explained), this should be addressed immediately when the members next attend. There should be a clear limit to how many sessions can be skipped. If members exceed that limit, they may need to be expelled from the group.

As the group progresses, members often develop a positive feeling of belonging. Eventually, the group may develop enough cohesiveness so that it may function as a transitional bridge (Bergart, 1986) that allows members to develop more intimate relationships. Emotional intimacy, however, may also create difficulties. When members identify with other's emotions or thought processes, they may experience painful reactions to their own abuse. These reactions may motivate them to address and begin to work through their own victimization. However, members may withdraw from the group if their own emotions become too distressful. Although the leader should encourage group cohesiveness, members should also be encouraged to separate their own distress from that of others. As members develop appropriate emotional boundaries, they can feel close enough to experience genuine connection with others but separate enough to feel like distinct individuals.

Themes related to the leader's control and status will likely emerge during the early phase (Bergart, 1986; Schulman, 1979). Statements about past therapists, physicians, teachers, landlords, and other authority figures may reflect a hidden theme of anger or fear regarding the group leader. As the leader analyzes these references, mediations can be planned. For example, after Twyla had discussed her "power hungry" boss, the leader commented, "I wonder how powerless you feel in this group, especially with me?" Members will likely respond with comments such as "You are not like those other people" or "I trust you." Although members' responses may be guarded, the leader's comments serve to encourage reflection about the leader's role and behavior. In later phases, the leader can encourage more in-depth discussions regarding the leader's authority and its implications. However, in this phase, the tenuous relationships within the group and with the leader may seem too fragile to survive open conflict.

THERAPIST AS MESSENGER
IN THE EARLY PHASE

During this and remaining phases, the therapist should model clear boundaries by starting and stopping on time, being assertive when appropriate, listening to members' painful revelations without appearing overwhelmed, and refusing to collude with a member or subgroup. Active listening may also be modeled by empathically reflecting and reframing content. For example, the leader may reflect, "As I've been listening to you, I remembered how you described your family role. I wonder if this is what you are really talking about?" Comments such as this demonstrate that the therapist has listened carefully and has searched for meaning beyond what has been said. Likewise, the leader models openness to feedback by inviting members to assess her or his leadership and by responding to feedback with acceptance and respect.

The teaching aspect of the messenger function should decrease significantly during the early phase of the group. If sessions become too topic centered, the therapist may be viewed more as a teacher than a therapist. If it is necessary to impart information, the therapist should label it as a minilecture. For example, the therapist may say, "Let's take time out for a minilecture about shame." After the information is given, the therapist may say something like "Okay, that is the end of the lecture. Let's get back to our therapy group." Minilectures or handouts about topics such as shame, the "child within," assertive behavior, and methods of problem solving can be helpful in this phase. Lessons are best reinforced when illustrated by group experience. For example, the leader gave the group information about boundaries and subsequently Dorie displayed a clear boundary. The leader reinforced this by saying, "You know, Dorie, when you just told Twyla that you were not responsible for her anger, you were showing good boundaries. These are the boundaries described in the handout I gave the group last week."

THERAPIST AS MEMBER
IN THE EARLY PHASE

As the group progresses, numerous and complex dynamics occur from moment to moment. Because the leader cannot observe and analyze every dynamic, the leader must remember that important dynamics will repeat themselves if they need attention. As the group progresses and the leader's attachment to the members increases, the leader may feel hurt or angry when members share painful experiences. It may be helpful to express those feelings on the client's behalf. For example, the leader may say, "Ann, when you shared what your brother did to you, I felt so angry at him. Do you experience anger toward him?" As the leader experiences and acknowledges personal emotional reactions, she or he must not only be empathic but also objective enough to function as the group leader. If the leader's reactions seem more related to personal issues (e.g., something reminds her of her own family), the leader should refrain from sharing comments until understanding the impact of that personal issue. A support network is essential to help the leader cope with feelings about personal issues that have been triggered. The therapy group must never be used for the leader's personal work.

The leader may have mixed feelings about having an authoritative position in the group. Although members may see the leader as powerful, he or she may at times feel quite powerless. The leader must continually survey personal cognitive and emotional reactions to being in this authoritative position and must diligently clarify boundaries around the leader role to "own" the power ascribed therein (Abney et al., 1992).

❏ The Middle Phase of Group

As the group moves into the middle phase, emotional connections should be well established and, as a result, members should feel more free to explore personal empowerment and autonomy. As members experience personal power, they often explore issues regarding the leader's power. At some point during this phase, they will likely confront the leader. After this and other confrontations, members can better understand their personal power and realize that relationships can be maintained even if conflicts occur.

Sessions 10 through 18: Struggles abounded during the middle phase. The conflict about Angie's relapse had many ramifications—especially regarding trust. Everyone seemed to be very needy, and the leader experienced difficulty balancing individual member needs with the needs of the group as a whole. Eventually, Ann confronted the leader by angrily blaming her for not "making sure everyone's needs were addressed." Initially caught off guard, the leader responded somewhat defensively by holding the group responsible. After consultation with her supervisor, the leader returned the next week and acknowledged her defensiveness. She then encouraged the group members to ventilate their anger about that or any other issues pertaining to her past behavior. Only Kate refrained from giving the leader feedback. Instead, she identified with the leader, saying, "It must be hard to be in your position." After the confrontation with the leader, the group seemed freer to express anger about many issues. A frequent "anger" topic focused on family of origin. In the midst of one of these discussions, Twyla disclosed her own daughter's abuse, and the group was highly supportive. About that time, Dorie began having more severe headaches and even some blackouts. During one group session, she ran out of the room and the leader found her in the bathroom having a flashback. Dorie resumed regular individual therapy and thereafter began using the group more effectively.

THERAPIST AS MONITOR AND MEDIATOR IN THE MIDDLE PHASE

The leader can learn a great deal about the power dynamics of the group by observing and analyzing how time is used. The division of time often indicates how the group will meet members' needs. Issues regarding time and attention can be assessed through questions such as:

"Do you need to be aggressive in order to be heard?"

"If you tend to be a passive member, do you expect to be drawn out, should you be responsible for asking for help?"

"Do you feel you have the right to block a dominant member from taking time?"

The group members should subsequently clarify how they can best manage time so all members' needs can be addressed. On occasion, the leader may need to limit an individual member's time so others' needs may be addressed. Some members may feel cutoff or rejected by these limitations and blame the leader for not taking care of their individual needs (Brandt, 1989). As with other issues, the leader should promote a process discussion regarding limitations.

Whenever a power theme emerges, the leader may draw attention to her or his role by remarking, "You have been talking about how powerless you feel in other relationships. I wonder how powerless you feel in group with me"; "When I said this to you right now I wonder if you felt anger toward me"; or "You know when you first came to group you had such high hopes that this would be helpful. I wonder if you are feeling disappointed that the group has not been more helpful or that maybe I could be doing more." These statements encourage members to reflect on the leader's behavior, and, perhaps, to confront the leader regarding her or his effectiveness.

The leader, when confronted, should react in an open and nondefensive manner. This is usually easier when the confrontation is rather benign. A member may ask, "I was wondering why you didn't do something when Kate left the room last week." The leader may respond to either the content or the meaning of the question. To search for the meaning of the question the leader may ask, "Are you feeling some anger or disappointment about that?" Other members may then be invited into the interaction by inquiring, "Did others of you feel angry or disappointed about my lack of action?" After discussion of members' emotional reactions and the resulting group dynamics, the leader can then respond to the content of the original question. Overall, the therapist must give the message "I am open to hearing your concerns and will respond directly to them. We can discuss and negotiate change in this group system."

Some leader confrontations are not so benign. If the confrontation is attacking or derogatory, the leader must model appropriate boundaries and must not allow herself or himself to be victimized. For example, when Angie confronted the leader, she said, "You are a cold bitch." If such attacking language is used, the leader must encourage the use of a more constructive, respectful language, using statements such as "I am open to hearing criticism but will not allow name calling or disparaging remarks. Please discuss, in respectful language using 'I' statements, your difficulties with my behaviors." Members may then reframe their criticism so that resolution can occur. If a member simply needs to vent anger, the leader may mediate appropriate boundaries by encouraging the member to discuss her personal reactions without making derogatory comments about others. If the attacking member does not respond to limits, the leader may need to interrupt the group by having all other members leave the room briefly or for a period of time. The angry member thus gets an opportunity to regain control of her behavior and the group can then resume with safety assured. Above all, safety within the group must be maintained and confrontations should ultimately be helpful to the group process.

A constructive confrontation of the group therapist may introduce a revolutionary change of members' beliefs regarding those in power (Yalom, 1985). Instead of believing "I must take what comes to me," members may learn, "I can confront others, even those in power, and empower change." Constructive confrontations may also clarify the boundary between the leader's and the members' roles. Members (as with children in healthy families where parental roles are clear and stable) may then feel more empowered to grow and change. With appropriate leader interventions, members can also learn how to confront each other constructively. The leader should intervene when disrespect is apparent but refrain from action when respectful confrontation occurs. By not acting, the leader indicates, "You can handle this. You do not need my intervention." By intervening in disrespectful interactions, the leader indicates that destructive anger will be managed and safety will be protected. For example, during an angry conflict, the leader may encourage respectful communication and clarify the content of communication by saying, "Angie, would you restate what you just said so Kate can better understand what is important to you?" and "Kate, are you understanding what is important to Angie?" This type of intervention keeps the confrontation focused on content so the members can resolve the problem at hand. Appropriate leader action (or nonaction) may help members eventually trust in their ability both to resolve conflict and to generalize that skill to outside relationships.

Leaders can help members trust their ability to resolve conflict inside and outside group.

As anger is expressed, members will likely display varying reactions. Some easily express anger while others are frightened of and avoid it. Members who depend on their anger to give them some sense of power are at risk of hurting other members. Those frightened of anger are likely to withdraw or even quit group when anger is experienced among members. These types of reactions often relate to family-of-origin issues. Certain members invariably remind others of a mother, father, sibling, or even the perpetrator. For example, Dorie felt anger toward Kate, who acted "like my sweet mother," and Twyla became angry when Angie acted "just like my spoiled little sister." As members processed this transferential anger, they began to understand not only their current relationships with their families of origin, but also how their families have influenced their beliefs and values.

As the middle phase progresses, the leader may observe many messages and roles that were likely influenced by members' families of origin. Members who were scapegoated in their families often emerge as scapegoats in the group; those who were caretakers care for other members; the family hero may vie for the leadership position; and the family clown provides comic relief. As the therapist observes the enactment of these dynamics, she or he can encourage discussion by asking, "Kate, do you think you are caretaking in the group the same way you did in your family?" or "Dorie, do you try to hide in here like you hide in your family?" Members who learn to recognize and understand these roles and how they have become automatic patterns of behavior can begin to experiment with alternative roles and behaviors. Some members may be encouraged to reconnect with certain family members as a way to overcome their position as victim (Deighton & McPeek, 1985). For example, Angie began to meet her mother for lunch (without her father) and Ann confronted her brother about his abusive behavior. Dorie, who realized that her family's teasing comments were actually emotionally abusive, behaved more assertively by refusing to accept such comments. Other members may be encouraged to establish more distance from their families. For example, Kate established clearer boundaries with her family by discontinuing her Sunday family gatherings. As members reframe their beliefs about their families of origin, most realize that their families will not reach the ideal they had fervently sought. Members must then grieve over the fact that their "fantasy family" will never be.

Subgrouping often becomes more pronounced during the middle phase and warrants close observation and analysis. At times, subgroups may join together "for or against" the leader or an individual member, or they may become adversarial toward one another. To prevent divisiveness, the therapist must mediate by encouraging process discussions. She or he may ask members, "How does it feel for you that these two are becoming such good friends?" or "How has it felt for you not to be included in this threesome?" As the door is opened to such discussion, it will be possible to explore issues regarding rivalry among members; this should lead to discussion of family-of-origin rivalries. Because such conflicts were often kept secret or left unresolved in members' families of origin, these process discussions may disrupt long-standing patterns regarding denial or avoidance of conflict. (Further discussion of destructive subgrouping is found in chapter 5.)

THERAPIST AS MESSENGER
IN THE MIDDLE PHASE

Modeling respect is especially important when conflict occurs. Self-respect is modeled by asserting clear boundaries and by blocking disrespectful communication. The therapist models respect of others when she or he encourages the expression of divergent opinions and emotions. The therapist should be open and responsive to both positive and negative member feedback.

When the leader assesses the need for education regarding topics such as assertiveness, conflict resolution, shame, intimacy, or boundaries, the use of handouts is especially helpful. If a group is having extreme difficulty with certain problems or patterns of interaction, an educational time-out may be advisable. One to four education sessions may be set aside for intensive education about specific topics. At times, it may be beneficial for someone other than the group therapist to conduct this education break so that the group leader's role as therapist will be clearly maintained.

Theoretical discussions of transference issues, especially regarding anger at the therapist, may be very helpful (Abney et. al, 1992). The therapist may also describe transference as a "group developmental" issue. As members become "older," more advanced, and empowered, they no longer need to depend on the leader alone to protect their power or to affirm their goodness or importance.

THERAPIST AS MEMBER
IN THE MIDDLE PHASE

For the therapist, the most personally challenging aspect of the middle phase of group is likely the leader confrontation. When a subgroup or the whole group confronts a leader, the leader can be frightened and even hurt. If the leader is open to learning about personal aspects, she or he should be able to receive critical information from the group and accept it constructively rather than defensively. It may be helpful for the leader to remember the importance of such confrontations and congratulate herself or himself after surviving one.

The leader's reactions to confrontation as well as other personal reactions may provide clues to salient group dynamics. The therapist should continually ask herself or himself, "What are my feelings telling me about what is happening in the group?" By such analysis, the leader should be able to monitor the deeper dynamics within the group. For example, if the leader experiences fear in reaction to a member's anger, other members are likely to be frightened as well. Despite the leader's fear, she or he should acknowledge it openly: "You know, I feel some fear when you are talking the way you are." Statements like this may prompt a fruitful discussion for the entire group.

During the middle phase, the leader may be distressed by the pace of the group, especially as individual members begin to complain about their perceived lack of progress. Because the leader is central to the group, immobility may mean the leader is stuck in her or his own personal life or professional development. The leader should honestly assess if any personal issues are blocking the group process and discuss this with the support group or a supervisor so that personal struggles do not impede the therapeutic process.

❏ The Advanced Phase of Group

Interactions of advanced groups are characterized by deep trust, strong connections, and open sharing. Advanced group behavior can occur within a few months of the group's beginning or may not occur for some time. A built-in ending/renewal time may motivate members to work more intensely as well as force them to assess their readiness for closure. We ask members in our groups to make 6-month commitments. Members may renew for another 6 months after the initial 6 months, or discontinue therapy. If most members in a group choose to recommit to the group, they may move into advanced behavior fairly quickly thereafter. If, however, most do not recommit, new members may need to be added. After adding new members, some groups maintain their momentum and behave as an advanced group, while other groups revert to the behavior of an earlier phase. Yalom (1985) suggests that members be added if the membership falls to five members or below.

> Sessions 18 through 24: As group members became closer to one another, more vulnerable sharing occurred about a variety of issues. A new struggle occurred between Twyla and Ann. Both had met the same man at a social function and became interested in pursuing a relationship. Twyla later attended a party with him not knowing that Ann was also interested in him. Ann felt anger and betrayal despite the fact that Twyla was unaware of Ann's interest. With further exploration, Ann discovered some transference dynamics regarding an older sister and the "sick" competition they had for their brother, the perpetrator. As Twyla and Ann conflicted, sessions were spent analyzing group dynamics. During these process groups, Kate was able to recognize and modify her caretaking role, and Ann was able to allow the conflict with Twyla without feeling responsible; this was a significant change from her family-of-origin role. Twyla was able to understand Ann's point of view and did not need "to make her see it my way." Angie and Dorie stayed involved in the group despite their intense fear of conflict. This was a great change for them both.

THERAPIST AS MONITOR
AND MEDIATOR IN THE ADVANCED PHASE

During the advanced phase, the therapist will likely observe deep intimacy and trust as members interact. If some remain outside of the intimate circle, the therapist should analyze whether the outside member has withdrawn and/or has been rejected. The ramifications for the outsider as well as for the group as a whole should be assessed. The therapist may intervene by saying, "Dorie, I've noticed that you don't seem to share as much as others and that you seem distant from the group. Can you share with us how you see your role in here?" After a response, a similar question about Dorie's role could be posed to the group. Although this may seem like a potentially shaming kind of statement, members likely experience more shame when they are left out or not directly involved. The group should receive the clear message that connection among all members is desirable.

The questions mentioned above are examples of the kind of process sharing that should occur during the advanced phase. Outside topics are less important than "here and now" group experiences, and entire group sessions may be spent discussing specific intermember behaviors. Because the topic for discussion is members' reactions to the present group experience, members can learn invaluable information about themselves. To continue with the above example, Dorie responded to the leader's comment by saying, "I just have the feeling that what I say isn't as important as what others say." The leader then asked, "Are there any members that especially make you feel that way?" Dorie responded by revealing her unexpressed anger regarding Twyla. Because Twyla had often suggested that Dorie read about emotions so she could better understand her physical symptoms, Dorie felt that Twyla had been judging her and "looking down" on her. Twyla in turn felt attacked, cried, and stated that Dorie misunderstood her. Dorie then felt like a perpetrator. The remaining members expressed a mixture of anger and sympathy toward Dorie. The leader continued by asking Twyla, "Has this kind of reaction happened elsewhere?" Twyla then recounted complaints others had about her controlling behavior. The leader asked the same of Dorie who discussed the shame she experienced whenever she acted assertively. Members outside of the conflict were also engaged when they were asked, "What was it like for you to watch this conflict?" Angie responded, "It was horrible, I felt just like I did when my parents fought. I wanted to run." Angie, however, was able to stay in the room throughout the interaction and learned she could observe conflict and not fulfill the need to escape. Depth processing should involve all group members, whether they are central to the topic or not. As members experience this type of processing, long-standing family patterns regarding secrecy, boundaries, and respect may be challenged. Members' relationships with one another deepen as they are assured that intimacy can be maintained even when anger and shame are processed.

The leader can encourage process discussions like the one above via *focus switches* (Yalom, 1985, p. 151). This method allows attention to be switched from an outside issue to an inside issue (focus on conflict with a boss is switched to conflict with the leader) or a past issue to a present issue (focus on a member rejected by friends to member rejection by group members). In the above example, the therapist could have initiated an outside-to-inside process interaction regarding Twyla's controlling behavior as follows: "Twyla has mentioned others complaining about her controlling behavior. I'm wondering if any of you experience Twyla as controlling?" Or the therapist could switch focus from a past to present issue by saying, "Kate, you have talked so much about how you had to parent your siblings. Do you think you are behaving that way in group?"

A focus shift may also turn the attention from a member's problem to the group as a whole. For example, Ann was discussing the fact that her sister had been recently diagnosed as clinically depressed. She cried as she recounted how her whole family "is a mess." Instead of keeping the focus on Ann, the leader decided to shift the focus to the group as a whole. Before shifting the focus away from Ann to the group as a whole, the leader first clarified the reason for the shift, saying, "Ann, I'd like to shift the focus for a bit. It feels like something important is happening in the group that could shed light on what you are sharing." The leader then said, "You all seem very sad as Ann has been talking. I'm wondering how much you are feeling for Ann or if you are actually taking on Ann's pain. Can you tell which is Ann's pain and which is yours?" After the group processed, the therapist returned to Ann to assess whether or not she needed further group time. Any focus shift from an individual member to the group as a whole should be respectful of the individual member's needs.

The most productive mediations often occur when the therapist encourages processing of current group behavior. In the above example, the therapist had observed enmeshment as Ann was sharing. When the group analyzed "whose pain belongs to whom," their minds held fresh their personal experience with enmeshment. If such process comments are made without evidence, they will be ineffective in the same way that insights in individual therapy are ineffective if they are not grounded in content or behavior.

In this phase, the functioning group will likely be perceived as a healthy pseudo-family (Courtois, 1988; Delvey, 1982). The nourishing and accepting environment of group may foster changes that allow damage from unhealthy family experiences to be healed. The potential healing aspects of this atmosphere can be recognized and reinforced by the leader when she or he makes comments such as "I am very pleased about your commitment to the group through all the struggles. That shows your ability to care about yourself and one another" or "You could not be talking about this if you didn't trust the group enough to take some risks." Such statements highlight the group's capabilities to develop and maintain intimacy. In beginning groups, members share doubts about their ability to feel close to anyone. In experiencing the intimacy of the advanced phase, they may realize, "I am close to the members in group so I can be close to some people. There are safe people in the world." As intimacy increases in group, friendships among members will likely continue to grow. The rule of no secrets is more important now than ever. If the therapist observes evidence of secrecy regarding group issues, intervention should be clear and decisive, using statements such as "Twyla, you looked like you know more about what Ann is sharing than just what she is telling us. Are you aware of any other information that we should know about?" Statements like this give members the message that secrecy is not in the best interest of the group or of any particular member.

In the advanced phase, the group can most effectively function as a corrective milieu in which members can repair their hurts and losses. As they heal, members can practice new behaviors that may be generalized outside of group. For example, Dorie spent months attempting to set up new boundaries with her mother, who continued to be verbally abusive. As she became more assertive within the group, Dorie began to set new limits with her mother as well. Likewise, as Twyla was able to allow herself to be less aggressive in the group, friends commented that she was easier to live with.

As members experience changes such as these, they may feel an uncomfortable "in-betweenness." Long-held beliefs and behaviors no longer fit, but new beliefs and behaviors are still unfamiliar. This experience may be analogous to moving from an old familiar house to a new, more functional house. Getting used to a new house takes time and energy, but eventually an adjustment takes place.

By suggesting leaderless group meetings, the therapist may reinforce members' changes, as well as their readiness to discontinue therapy. If members can agree on rules and roles, leaderless groups can help them realize that they can continue to help themselves and others without a therapist present. Increased autonomy also forces members to consider their competence and readiness to face life without group. The readiness for departure should be carefully assessed personally by each member and through feedback from the group. Feedback regarding departure from group may be formalized (asking one member to receive as other members give feedback) or the feedback may occur as free-floating group discussions. Members in the advanced phase likely trust each other to give and receive honest, positive, and helpful feedback. They can then receive valuable information regarding accomplishments and needed changes. This open feedback can serve as a reality check, allowing members to assess which goals are realistic and which are not. Members' goals such as the desire to have a loving family, a changed personality, or outstanding achievements may never be realized, and they need to be ready to accept that possible reality.

THERAPIST AS MESSENGER IN THE ADVANCED PHASE

During the advanced stage, the therapist's respect for the group as the primary healing force must be apparent. The leader continues to share insights and observations as group members are encouraged to share their insights and observations with one another.

Rather than lecture, the therapist can encourage discussion during which members share their own views. By this time, the group should realize that the therapist does not have all the answers. Instead, members can look to one another or themselves for answers.

THERAPIST AS MEMBER IN THE ADVANCED PHASE

As the group experiences deeper intensity, the therapist will likely experience deeper emotional involvement. At times it may be a personal struggle for the leader to stay distant enough to be objective. Questions such as "How does one form an adult relationship with a parent?"; "How does one balance individual needs with the needs of the relationship?"; and "How does one cope with issues of power and control?" may be a struggle for the leader personally and professionally. During the advanced group, the leader may be most tempted to set aside her or his professional role and jump into the discussion as an equal member. The leader may ask herself or himself, "What makes them less troubled than I?" or "Am I stable enough to be in the leader position?" At times, members may even risk intimacies beyond what the leader would risk. The leader may ask, "Could it be that members will become 'healthier' than I?" The support of colleagues or friends is crucial at this point. The leader must experience empathy while continuing to function as a messenger, monitor, and mediator.

❑ The Closure Phase

Groups should formally close if fewer than five members recommit. After a closure, either new members may be added or the few remaining members may blend with another group. In some groups, especially those that have committed through two or more series, all members may choose to discontinue therapy. These groups may wean themselves from therapy by meeting twice monthly, then monthly for a period of time, while other groups meet weekly until closure. After therapy is discontinued, group members may choose to continue to meet socially or for intermittent reunions with the therapist. Whatever structure is decided upon for closure, the group should have time to understand and adjust to closure. We advise at least four meetings to focus on closure issues.

THERAPIST AS MONITOR
AND MEDIATOR DURING CLOSURE

Discussion of closure forces members to make many choices, the most important of which is whether or not to continue with therapy. This choice is influenced by issues both outside and within the group. If members are coping well outside of group, have experienced some resolution regarding their families of origin, and have accepted the reality of the incest and its consequences, they will likely choose to discontinue. Internal group issues will also influence closure. If most members are leaving, those remaining must make a difficult choice. Do they stay in therapy even though their peers are leaving, or do they leave like everyone else? The therapist must emphasize the importance of individual choice and should encourage feedback sessions as described in the previous section. Whatever the decision, the individual choice to stay or leave must be respected.

As choice is explored, grief regarding the loss of group is also experienced. Therapists should encourage emotional expression of this loss and other past losses. This review of past abandonments, rejections, deaths, and "little girl" losses can be quite moving and often allows the entire group to experience feelings related to grief and loss. Because of the painful emotions, the group needs encouragement to continue to experience unresolved griefs as well as the current loss of group therapy. Group members may react to the grief process by reverting to earlier forms of coping (Rose, 1989) and then fear that they will be unable to maintain the gains they have made. The leader should reassure by clarifying that these "setbacks" need not be permanent.

Often groups plan their own ending celebration or ritual for the last therapy session. The way the group ends varies with the type of group. Some groups choose to have a party complete with gifts and food. Other groups choose to give imaginary gifts or awards that symbolize members' progress. Whatever closing ritual is chosen, the ritual should affirm the deep respect members hold for one another and serve as an affirmation of the healing that has occurred. Each member should acknowledge how she has changed, and at the same time acknowledge the loss of the group.

THERAPIST AS MESSENGER
DURING CLOSURE

The leader should model the concept that transitions may be both celebrated and grieved. As she or he models self-disclosure about her or his own loss regarding the group, members will likely feel more free to disclose their own feelings of loss. Although members' sense of loss is likely more intense, the feeling of loss is there for all.

During teaching breaks, the leader should offer time for members to evaluate their group experience and discuss the meaning of the group to them (Drews & Bradley, 1989). Members may also benefit from information about the stages of grieving, the negative effects of unresolved grief, and information about life transitions. They should understand that transitions are inevitable in everyone's life and that proper grieving can help one cope. Members who have never experienced proper closure to any interpersonal relationship may need to be taught how to say "good-bye."

Information about aftercare is also necessary. It is helpful to review other community programs and support networks available that will help members continue their growth. Each member should make a commitment to the group to maintain and continue growth by clarifying follow-up plans.

THERAPIST AS MEMBER DURING CLOSURE

The experience of having worked with a group from the beginning to completion should allow the leader to perceive the healing power of these groups. As the group members experience issues of grief and loss, so may the leader. The leader likely has become connected with each member and the group as a whole and will experience personal grief. The leader may also be tempted to keep the group going because it works so well. However, it is important to act as a "good parent" and encourage appropriate autonomy by launching group members with care and wishing them the best. The leader's own unresolved grief issues will likely surface during this time, and the leader may need a support network to assist in resolving those issues. If these personal issues are left unaddressed, the leader may unconsciously discourage open discussion of grief and loss in the group.

During closure, the leader might find it especially difficult to clarify boundaries and roles. The leader may be asked by members to function as an individual therapist or as a friend. We advise that the leader maintain the role as therapist for a long period after the end of therapy (1 to 2 years) before considering friendships with any member. Members need the leader in a therapy role so the incorporation of a "positive parent" can stay with them.

5

Special Issues

This chapter describes special problems that may occur in some groups. The three sections address these problems as they relate to the group as a whole, interactions within the group, and individual member issues. We continue to emphasize the perspectives of power, goodness, and importance and the therapist's functions of monitor, mediator, messenger, and member. We introduce new members in the group vignettes.

❏ The Group as a Whole

STUCK OR RESISTANT GROUPS

The therapist began to dread 2:30 on Friday afternoon, the time her "stuck" group met. Despite many attempts to get the group going, members only briefly interacted, falling into extended silences. When members did interact it was often through the leader. Members attended group sporadically, were often tardy, and tended to be highly guarded. Even after months, there was mistrust and little connection among the members. The group expressed hopelessness and the general theme seemed to be "This group can't help. Nothing can."

Therapist as Monitor and Mediator

Resistance (or becoming seemingly "stuck") are common to the group therapy process for a variety of reasons (Schulman, 1979). In some cases, the leader may have avoided confronting issues that the group seemed resistant to discuss. By avoiding those issues, the leader communicated to the group that she or he went along with their resistance. In other cases, the leader may not have empowered members to help each other. Perhaps the therapist chose topics for discussion and/ or diverted the group's attention from member topics. If this scenario occurs regularly, members may stop introducing their own topics. The therapist may then mistakenly interpret members' passive behavior as an indication of their need for even more direction. Instead of becoming more directive, however, the therapist should become less active. To become less active, the therapist may state, "I need to change my approach to this group. I have been too directive when you, as a group, should be establishing the direction." When the leader takes a less directive role, members will likely assume more control and engage in the process of helping themselves and each other.

Poor attendance, tardiness, or lack of involvement may also reflect the members' lack of hopefulness about the group's effectiveness. Initially, the therapist may have conveyed a hopeful attitude, but eventually she or he also doubted the group's helpfulness. To encourage hope, the leader must first believe in the potential effectiveness of the group and then impart that hope to the members. To change the atmosphere of hopelessness, each member must be able to believe in the potential effectiveness of the group and state those beliefs openly. If members cannot attain some level of hope, changes in group membership may be needed. Optimistic members could be added and/or some current members could be transferred to a better functioning (or more positive) group.

In addition to exploring hope, the leader may also explore the issue of trust. At times, extreme resistance may indicate that members do not have confidence in the leader's skills or style (Corey, 1985). The leader should ask,

- "Do you trust me as your leader?"
- "Who do you believe is responsible for making this group work?"
- "Do you think I trust you to help each other?"
- "How would you rate the trust level of this group?"
- "Do you believe you can help each other?"

If members are hesitant to answer such questions directly, they may write responses to the questions. When written or verbal responses indicate a lack of trust, the leader should encourage members to brainstorm together about how trust can be enhanced. The content of this brainstorming may not be as important as the process of having members work together to enhance trust.

Therapist as Messenger

The leader must demonstrate a hopeful attitude, yet express concern or frustration when appropriate. The leader thus models her or his "unstuckness" by openly communicating hopes and frustrations about the group. Members, as a result, may feel more free to express their own honest reactions to the group. The leader should also demonstrate her or his "demand-for-work skills" (Schulman, 1979, p. 65) by supportively and assertively encouraging the members to help each other. The leader should not appear to be working harder than the members. If improvement does not occur, a leader may request individual meetings with each member and her individual therapist. These meetings serve not only to highlight the importance of each member, they may also allow the leader and the member to assess the group's potential effectiveness for that member.

Stuck groups may need an education break to study the 4 Rs (respect, reflect, respond, and receive) and make plans to implement them better. They may also discuss hope and its role in personal growth and change.

Therapist as Member

The leader in this type of group will likely be frustrated or angry about the group but also puzzled about why the group is not effective. Because the group's "stuckness" may reflect the leader's own stuckness, the leader must assess her or his personal issues. The leader should share frustrations with a support network and then strategize about how to share those frustrations with the therapy group in a helpful way.

THE HOSTILE GROUP

A 7-month-old group of five members was an especially lively group. They valued openness and honesty and could readily confront each other. The therapist was relieved when, during the 5th month, she survived the group's rather hostile confrontation. She assumed that the group would then be freer to express emotions other than anger. However, during the 6th month, hostility became more intense, especially after one member was arrested for writing bad checks. This member believed she had been treated unfairly by the legal system. Subsequently, other members began to describe injustices they had endured. The anger seemed to build on itself and members began arguing with one another. At times, the leader had difficulty controlling the arguments—especially when they continued after the group's formal time structure. Although the anger seemed to enliven the group and members asserted that they argued because they "cared," the therapist felt concerned about the group's potential destructiveness.

Therapist as Monitor and Mediator

Incest survivors may not have learned how to express anger constructively. Suppressing or abusing may be the only models they have had for dealing with anger (Swink & Leveille, 1986). Some groups may include a disproportionate number of members who tend to express anger in abusive ways. Unlike the stuck group, members in these groups actively interact with one another. Because of this interaction, the leader may mistakenly hold back and become almost peripheral to the group process. The leader is, however, essential to the health of the group (Yalom, 1985) and should intervene consistently and assertively, especially when members are abusive in any way. For example, Kathy told Helen, "You make me sick. You are just wasting your life at that job." The leader, who interpreted the comment as an attack, stopped the interaction and asked Helen and Kathy to share their feelings. Kathy expressed anger at the leader for controlling her and defended her right to share her feelings of concern for Helen. Helen reported feeling attacked but believed she needed "a kick."

> *The leader must consistently intervene to maintain safety.*

In this interchange, the leader respected Kathy's right to speak freely by allowing some expression of anger but intervened when Helen was emotionally attacked. If the leader does not consistently intervene to maintain safety, members may ignore or undermine her or his interventions when they do occur. If this happens, a supervisor or consultant may need to be invited into the group to support the leader's authority, or a coleader may be permanently added to the group.

At times, aggression takes place outside the formal group setting. Some members may even wait for the leader to leave and then hold postgroup meetings to express their feelings without the constraints of the leader. Obviously, the leader cannot control members' activities outside of the group's time structure, but members may be advised against such interactions because of their potential dangers. If the group ignores such admonitions, the leader may, as a last resort, disband the group because such destructive behavior cannot be sanctioned by the leader or the employing agency.

The leader should keep in mind that hostility or aggressiveness may indicate the existence of underlying feelings (Corey, 1985). To encourage recognition of these underlying emotions, various interventions can be implemented. For example, the leader may ask, "If you were feeling sad how do you think you would react to what Jane is saying?" or "How do you think shame may be fueling your anger right now?" The leader may also intervene during a confrontation by saying, "Amy, you looked sad when Helen said that. Are you feeling sadness along with the anger?" Employing exercises that recognize "little girl" or "parts of self" may also assist members in understanding the origin of their anger and in recognizing other emotions. Through such exploration, members may discover that they use hostility to feel powerful or important, to mask shame and vulnerability, or to avoid intimacy.

Because freedom of expression is so highly valued, these types of groups may demand that all members actively challenge one another. However, this may promote confrontation instead of support. When asked about their confrontational style, some members may describe it as caring or supportive. They may also acknowledge their inability to show support in a nonconfrontational manner. Some may say, "I just can't be gentle with others" or "People know I care when I get angry." Other members may have the ability to be gently supportive but feel that the group rules will not allow that kind of sharing. To encourage safe connections among members, the leader may need to orchestrate interactions by encouraging some types of communication and blocking others. Members may be encouraged to use "I" messages, speak in soft voices, or frame responses in supportive language. A leader should stop members if they are shouting or using accusatory language. At times, the leader may even limit some members from interacting for a part or all of a session. Members who are accustomed to behaving hostilely may learn a great deal from taking an observing role. Process discussions may help members learn how hostility and aggression affect their ability to connect with others in the group. If intermember hostility is very intense, the therapist may rule that anger must be mediated by the leader (O'Hare & Taylor, 1983).

Sometimes the members' hostility relates to the leader's style or emotional availability. In some cases, the leader may have reacted defensively to a member's confrontation and thus seems emotionally defensive and unreachable. In other cases, the leader may value a confrontational style of therapy and, subtly or openly, promote intermember confrontation. This type of leader may encourage a "hot seat" approach through which members are confronted until they display vulnerability. This leader type may also have modeled angry responses in earlier situations and inadvertently encouraged the group to respond with anger. Conversely, a leader may be frightened of anger and unconsciously refrain from confronting the destructive anger within the group. To explore those issues with the group, the leader should encourage process discussions and may ask, "Do you have unresolved anger toward me?"; "Does my leadership style promote confrontation?"; "Are you hesitant to confront me?"; or "Have you witnessed me displaying emotions other than anger?" As with other problem areas, many of these difficulties may have been prevented if group selection had included members with the ability to display a range of emotions.

Therapist as Messenger

The leader should model assertiveness by being honest about feeling angry and assertive in her or his expressions. The leader should also model the "softer" emotions by displaying gentle and nourishing responses. If members can observe such a range of responses and see positive outcomes, they may attempt such responses themselves.

Using education breaks to teach assertiveness can be very helpful. Members should be assured that they have a right to feel angry, but not to behave in abusive manners. It may be helpful to interrupt the group process and conduct an assertiveness training seminar. (Please refer to Jehu's 1988 book, *Beyond Sexual Abuse: Therapy with Women Who Were Childhood Victims*, for a description of one assertiveness training format.) Members may also need education about recognizing and experiencing various emotions. The leader may encourage members to analyze the pros and cons of expressing emotions other than anger, and have them practice recognizing and expressing emotions other than anger. Some specific informative content on shame may also be advised, because these members may experience shame beneath their anger. Discussion of members' family-of-origin patterns regarding anger and fear of intimacy may also be helpful.

Therapist as Member

The therapist, on rare occasions, may be physically attacked by an extremely hostile member. If this occurs, the member who assaulted the leader should be expelled from the group and experience appropriate legal consequences. After these actions are completed, the leader and the remaining members need to process reactions to the assault thoroughly. Some members may have gotten angry and attempted to protect the leader, others may have fled from the room, and some may have frozen. During the processing time, members may analyze their typical reactions reactions to out-of-control anger. The leader must also process her or his own fear, anger, or shame. The leader may feel frightened about returning to the group or may be frightened about further victimization from the assaulting member. The leader should seek protection from the legal system and the agency so she or he can continue to function in the leader role.

THE HIGHLY TROUBLED GROUP

This group of six had been referred from a psychiatric hospital. All members shared an incest history of long duration, invasive abuse, and multiple perpetrators. Most were clinically depressed. Many knew each other from previous treatment settings and therefore seemed to trust one another. However, as time progressed, the level of trust varied greatly. During some sessions members shared intimately with one another. During others, they hardly spoke. Frequent hospitalizations caused attendance to be unpredictable. Self-destructive behavior was the norm and, at times, members would compare their numbers of suicide attempts or boast about other self-injurious behaviors such as driving recklessly. As a result, the therapist felt overwhelmed and confused.

Therapist as Monitor and Mediator

Most of the members in the example group believe that they have little or no control over their life circumstances. Many seem unable to make and/or act on decisions that result in positive outcomes. When the therapist speaks optimistically about members' abilities to control the direction of their lives, members may respond with cynicism. They may even confront the therapist by stating, "If there is hope, why don't I ever get better?" or "Why should I do positive things if it doesn't change the way I feel?" Despite members' pessimism, the leader should continue to highlight positive choices and reframe situations in a positive, hopeful, and realistic perspective. A hopeful perspective is necessary if the group is to be effective (Yalom, 1985).

Like other incest survivors, members in these groups often experience shame. Their level of shame, however, could be better described as self-hatred. This pattern of self-hatred and self-loathing is common in victims who were severely abused both sexually and emotionally (Briere, 1989). Although they may desire to be rid of these negative self-assessments as well as the associated memories and emotions, members may fear discussing those thoughts, memories, and emotions with the group. Some may have confronted these beliefs only to be overwhelmed by distressing memories and emotions. Others may have felt rejected after sharing details of their lives and have come to believe they "contaminate others" and cause them to leave the group. If this deep level of shame is to be confronted, members need to discuss their beliefs and emotions associated with shame. Because of their fears, however, the group's sharing varies from vulnerable openness to resistant or painfully uncomfortable silences.

A structured approach may be warranted. The group time may be divided so members can discuss chosen topics for a specific period of time. Members may request structured time-outs when distress becomes overwhelming. If activities are planned, the leader should discuss the purpose and content of each activity thoroughly. Members can then decide which activity would be most helpful. Topic- or activity-centered experiences may enhance consistency within each meeting. This should, in turn, enhance safety. Activities may include cognitive approaches such as having members write or verbalize more positive attitudes, clarify responsibilities regarding past behaviors, or label emotions and their accompanying thoughts. Visualizations or working with metaphors may also assist in labeling and working with emotions. Role plays to practice behavioral skills such as assertion may also be advised.

These and other activities should enhance group safety and encourage trust development. Because building trust in these groups is an extremely slow process, the leader must be prepared to give the time and attention necessary for a level of trust to develop. Once this occurs, the group will likely require less structure and guidance. If trust is to develop, rules about attendance must be strictly enforced. When members experience frequent hospitalizations, it may be difficult to have a core group of regularly attending members. In response, a quota may be enacted—for example, if fewer than four members are present, the group session is canceled. To maintain the quota, the therapist may request that hospitalized members attend group or that the group meet at the hospital.

Members' ability to trust and connect with one another is often thwarted by their inability to structure emotional boundaries. They may "take on" the problems of others and see themselves as failures when they cannot solve problems for each other. Thus, the emotional distress of one member may overwhelm others. When others share emotionally charged content, some may dissociate themselves from the entire experience. The leader should, therefore, regularly check with those listening in regard to their emotional reactions and boundaries. If others begin to show significant distress, the sharing may be interrupted until more appropriate boundaries can be structured. For example, when Connie cried as she shared emotions about a hurtful past incident, other members displayed strong emotions as well. The leader stopped the interaction and asked Connie what she most needed from the group. When she responded that what she needed was someone to listen, the leader coached the others to listen without thinking of solutions or their own problems, and without "taking on" Connie's emotions.

Whenever possible, it is most desirable to assess potential members' levels of dysfunction during the selection process. We have found it helpful to include members displaying varying degrees of dysfunction. If groups become too homogeneous in terms of dysfunction, negative attitudes may become the shared beliefs of the group and will be extremely difficult to change.

Therapist as Messenger

The therapist must behave respectfully and responsively toward members and should reinforce their value as human beings. Displaying respect is especially challenging when members' views are extremely negative. The therapist should be prepared to reflect and respond with regard to those views, but be mindful of not reinforcing them.

These groups may need to be more topic centered for periods of times. In addition to the approaches previously mentioned, the group may study topics such as hope, depression, and one's "right to commit suicide."

Therapist as Member

Because of members' suicidal threats and behaviors, leading these groups may produce anxiety. The leader may also become frustrated because maintaining hope is difficult in a very pessimistic environ-

Failure to change negative norms may actually reinforce dysfunction.

ment. The leader's beliefs about life and death, good and evil, and hope and despair are challenged. The leader must continually ask herself or himself whether the group appears more helpful than harmful. If the leader cannot assist the group to change the negative norms, the group may actually reinforce dysfunction. If this occurs, the leader, and the supervisory network, may need to decide whether or not to continue the group.

❏ Interactions Within Group

SUBGROUPING

This group of six had progressed well until their 3rd month, when an argument about group philosophy occurred. Three members wanted the therapist to take a more structured approach, as had been done in a self-help group they had belonged to; other members wanted things to continue unchanged. As time passed, this division became apparent, and each subgroup developed its own philosophy about group rules. Eventually, each subgroup arrived together and met separately as a subgroup after group. The leader felt caught in the middle and initiated many process discussions; however, no resolutions evolved. The group later disbanded with the subgroups intact.

Therapist as Monitor and Mediator

Subgroups, especially those with norms contrary to the leader's, can be especially problematic. Sometimes a number of members have been exposed to other recovery groups or therapy approaches. Confusion results if in one setting members are encouraged to express anger at the perpetrator but in another setting are told that anger is dysfunctional. The subgroup receiving advice contrary to the leader's often decides to confront the leader about her or his approach. These confrontations may be beneficial if the leader is open to hearing members' concerns and is flexible about aspects of her or his treatment approach. The goal of this discussion should be to negotiate an approach that is both beneficial to the group as a whole and agreeable to the therapist. To reach this consensus, members may simply need to understand the pros and cons of different approaches. If views cannot be reconciled, subgroup members need to decide if they can remain in the therapy group. After these negotiations, members need to recommit to the group's new approach, or leave the group.

Whatever decision is made about differing viewpoints, rules regarding outside group contacts need to be very clear. The leader may suggest a written contract indicating rules and consequences regarding member contacts outside of group. In extreme cases, the leader may suggest or require that certain subgroups not meet outside of group. Within group sessions the leader may request certain seating arrangements, dyad and triad work, or other specific interactional techniques. All these interventions are predicated on the assumption that members respect the leader's guidance. If not, their primary allegiance may remain with the subgroup.

Intermember trust is threatened by extreme subgrouping. Those members not part of a subgroup that regularly meets outside of group may believe they are being secretly discussed or even ridiculed. Some may feel shame or believe they are socially undesirable if they are not part of the subgroup's social contacts. The situation may remind them of earlier experiences regarding secrecy, betrayal, or exclusion. Some subgroup members may feel guilty about their separate contacts, and need to make decisions about loyalty. They may ask themselves, "Do I betray the subgroup by revealing our discussions to the whole group or do I remain loyal to the subgroup and keep secrets?" The leader must convince members that breaking this kind of secrecy is healthy for them and for the entire group. Members should be reminded that the conspiracy of silence that surrounds a subgroup, not the subgroup itself, is what can cause harm to members or to the group as a whole (Yalom, 1985).

Members of subgroups may have difficulty connecting with the group as a whole, especially when dividing lines exist from the very beginning. The leader may have selected members who are naturally divided along issues such as optimism versus pessimism, alcoholic versus nonalcoholic, previous therapy versus no previous therapy, married versus unmarried, or parents versus nonparents. The leader should promote open discussions regarding this diversity and encourage the group to develop rules to establish and reinforce cohesiveness. A cohesion plan with defined goals and time frames may be formulated. If goals are not met within the designated time frames, the group's future may be at risk.

A cohesion plan is also necessary when two existing groups are to be joined. In such instances, a leader must first be chosen. If the two groups have had the same therapist, that person can continue in the leader role and provide a unifying force for combining the two groups. However, if the two groups have had different therapists, we advise assigning a new leader to prevent divisive alliances. If a therapist new to both groups is not available, therapists of the existing groups will need to decide who should remain in the leader role for the newly combined group. The newly chosen leader may then conduct a pregroup training session to devise a cohesion plan.

A variation of subgroup dynamics may occur when a single member is involved with a therapist, sponsor, or mentor who is critical of the group approach. These members may feel torn between the group and the other helper. A cohesion plan may again be helpful. The group therapist, group member, and other helper(s) involved should meet to discuss how all may work together to best assist the member's recovery.

Therapist as Messenger

Because the leader needs to show respect for the group as a whole, it is imperative that she or he not side with any subgroup. This neutral position can be very difficult. We advise that the therapist be open about her or his desire to bridge all divisiveness. For example, the therapist may say, "It's almost like there are two groups here. I'm feeling frustrated about how to get you together." Perhaps as members respond to the therapist's openness, they can be more open about their struggles with their considerations of loyalty. The therapist should also model a willingness to receive positive and negative feedback, and an ability to negotiate resolutions regarding areas of concern.

The group may benefit from instruction regarding group systems and the effects of subgroups. The leader may map the existing group structure and discuss the implications of subgrouping for all involved. The group could then be subdivided into study groups (different in composition from the existing subgroups) to discuss family-of-origin or other relationship patterns that relate to the subgrouping problems.

Therapist as Member

The leader may be personally threatened or overwhelmed by a particular subgroup, especially if one subgroup confronts the leader about her or his attitudes or skills. The leader may even be tempted to deny the destructive aspects of the subgroup so it can remain "safely secretive"; this denial protects the leader from confrontation. Whatever the leader's fears, the use of a support network is crucial in enabling the leader to stay in the leadership role and not align with any subgroup. A healthy support network will help the leader decide where she or he needs to make changes or learn new skills. It also will reinforce or reassure the leader in areas where she or he is doing well.

DEVIANT MEMBERS AND SCAPEGOATING

Five members in a group of six were single, worked full time, and were active in the community. Their intellectual ability was above average and they had much therapy experience. One member, Kay, was among those who had much therapy experience, but was a single mother whose intellectual ability and socioeconomic status were noticeably different from the others. Kay felt out of place and often attacked the group for being "snobs." When Kay was absent, others would joke about her. The leader intervened when negative comments occurred, but was then accused of taking sides. The group did seem to work better when Kay was absent. All, including the leader, believed it would be helpful for Kay to leave the group.

Therapist as Monitor and Mediator

The example group displays a scapegoating pattern. Scapegoating is a method "by which the group can discharge anger arising from any source" (Yalom, 1985, p. 355) onto a member or members. Members in the scapegoat role are often socialized, by family and life experience, into such roles and may be ready volunteers for the scapegoating role (Schulman, 1979). Because incest survivors are often conditioned to see themselves as deviant (Hays, 1987), they may easily fall into this pattern. The scapegoating process, however, involves more than one member volunteering for this role. The group also colludes in this process and has some functional need for a scapegoat. The function of a scapegoating pattern may be difficult to analyze in incest groups because members may react strongly to perpetrator and victim roles. For example, as the scapegoat is emotionally victimized, others will likely experience guilt and anger about their own perpetrator role. This guilt may incite even more anger at the scapegoat for causing members to react so cruelly and the pattern becomes a repetitious cycle. Whenever this pattern occurs, the safety of all members is compromised. Only the leader may be able to change the pattern.

Before mediation, however, the leader should hypothesize about the causes of the scapegoating pattern. A common dynamic that perpetuates a scapegoating pattern is unexpressed anger at the leader (Yalom, 1985). It may be easier for a member to project displaced anger onto a deviant member who seems to "invite" such a response than onto the leader, who is perceived as powerful. To compound the problem, the leader may unconsciously encourage displacement of anger by criticizing or failing to protect the scapegoat. The scapegoating pattern may also relate to members' unresolved shame. Some members, to avoid facing their own shame, may continue to strike out at the deviant member. They may believe, "If I can concentrate on the bad qualities of others, I will not need to face all the badness in me."

In a scapegoating situation, it is nearly impossible to remain neutral. The leader will at some point need to make her or his views clear. When the leader hears negative comments like "I hope Kay won't come today," she or he is forced either to reinforce the comments by ignoring or agreeing with them, or to defend Kay. The leader's natural tendency may be to defend the scapegoat. However, this may only intensify members' anger at the scapegoat. Instead, the leader should focus on the group as a whole and view the scapegoating pattern as the group's way of offering a theme of concern (Schulman, 1979). To defend both Kay's and the group's integrity, the leader may begin a process discussion. For example, the leader, keeping in mind that the scapegoating pattern may reflect unexpressed anger at the leader, said, "I'm observing a scapegoating pattern between Kay and the group. I'd like to hear your views about my handling of this conflict between Kay and the rest of you." Some members responded by sharing their frustration about the leader's pretending the problem did not exist, while others were angry about using group time to talk about the scapegoating. Kay responded by crying and saying, "I don't understand why they don't seem to like me." The leader then explored the function of the pattern by saying, "Now I'd like to explore why this group needs this pattern. I'm wondering why the group needs someone to be angry with and why Kay is accepting the scapegoating role." The group responded by indicating they did not have to concentrate on themselves if they could focus on Kay. The leader then switched the focus by saying, "Kay, how did you handle this type of situation when you were growing up?" and "Mary, is your anger with Kay similar to your anger with your sister?" Kay cried as she related how she always seemed to fall into this role, and Mary lamented her aggressive behavior toward her younger sister. After the process discussions, the group agreed to view the scapegoating pattern as a signal that members are avoiding their own issues.

After such process discussions, the group can devise plans to change the scapegoating dynamic. If all members, including the scapegoat, devise a plan to correct the scapegoating pattern, they may establish a new group structure. For example, all members may agree to self-monitor rejecting statements or behavior and to respond immediately to the leader's interventions if it occurs. If the group is successful in changing a scapegoating pattern, the members may be able to change some basic beliefs about themselves. Beliefs such as "once a victim, always a victim" may be changed to "I need not always play a victim role." Likewise, beliefs about one's impact on others may be changed from "I am never a perpetrator" to "Even I can hurt others." Members may also learn that although people may hurt each other, with reparation, trust can still be achieved. Changing the scapegoating pattern in group may also influence changes in members' personal relationships. If interventions fail to change the scapegoating pattern, the deviant member may need to be reassigned to a different group or to individual therapy. This is an extreme solution, however, and should be the last option considered.

As is the case with other problems, prevention is the best approach to scapegoating. The leader should encourage early process discussions about members' economic, marital, or social status. Diversity could then be respected as unique qualities that could contribute to group learning. Members may brainstorm about what they might learn from the "deviant" member's unique qualities. Discussions about closeness and distance should also be encouraged. Leader comments such as "Which members do you feel safest with?" may encourage process discussions to occur before deviancy becomes destructive.

Therapist as Messenger

The leader must behave respectfully toward the group as a whole while at the same time refusing to collude with the scapegoat. This does not mean, however, that attacking behavior is tolerated. As mentioned in the discussion of a hostile group, the leader should act assertively to block any abusive communication. The leader, by blocking attacks toward the scapegoat, models how those in power can protect victims. Members' behavior may follow the leader's example and the scapegoating pattern may be tempered.

The group may need an educational time out to discuss the dynamics of scapegoating and the 4 Rs, and to brainstorm about ways to change behavior. Shame and anger may also be discussed.

Therapist as Member

Dealing with the scapegoating process is most difficult when the leader does not like the deviant member. The leader may consciously or unconsciously want her to leave the group and inadvertently reinforce the anger directed at the scapegoat. The leader also may be reinforcing the scapegoating process to avoid having the group's anger directed at herself or himself. Honest self-reflection and discussion are warranted.

DROPOUTS

> This group of eight had been meeting for 4 months. Members shared readily and seemed to have a high trust level. All members, including the leader, were shocked when Mary decided to leave the group before renewal time. She felt she had received enough help and was ready for a break. The discussion regarding Mary's departure was quite disruptive to the group process.

Therapist as Monitor and Mediator

Although attrition tends to occur most often in or during the early phases, it can occur at any time. Reasons for early termination vary but may include external factors: time or place, problems with intimacy, fear that group will make things worse, conflict between individual and group therapy, or deviancy (Yalom, 1985). From the beginning, expectations should be clarified regarding time commitment and group attendance. As mentioned previously, we expect members to make a 6-month commitment. If, for some reason, a member decides to leave before 6 months, that member should attend at least one more group to discuss or explain her decision to leave. A member who is ambivalent about leaving may need the group to help her with the decision. Other members may give feedback about issues that they believe that member still needs to address, or they may explore with that member how they as a group could be more helpful. After such discussions, the ambivalent member should clarify her commitment to the group. She should not be allowed to stay in the group if she cannot commit, because this disrupts group trust. On rare occasions, certain members may discuss leaving as a way to receive the group's time and attention. Such attention-seeking behavior should be acknowledged, discussed, and discouraged.

Members who leave prematurely should be encouraged to discuss their choice, but the group members should also have an opportunity to discuss their reactions. These discussions can allow all to have a sense of closure. If the member who is leaving refuses to meet with the group, the leader should request a letter that clarifies her reasons for leaving. At the very least, the leader should hold an "exit interview" with the departing member to discuss thoroughly the reasons for early departure. The leader should clarify with the departing member what information from the exit interview can be shared with the remaining group members.

When a member chooses to leave prematurely, the remaining members often feel responsible for causing the departure. If a member leaves as a result of a scapegoating pattern, the members who used her as a scapegoat need to confront their role in her departure. The leader should mediate discussions about guilt and self-forgiveness so that the remaining members can move on. It may be helpful for members to discuss how they will fill the function of the departing member's role and how the group identity will change after the member's departure. Members then have the opportunity to reassess their place in group. The leader may also encourage discussions about significance by asking, "How do you imagine the group would react if you left?" If member departure necessitates adding a new member, thorough discussion must precede the new member's admittance to prevent that person from being placed into "the dropout's" role.

To prevent member dropout, trust should be discussed regularly. Some members may feel deviant regarding their trust level, especially when they judge that others seem to be more trusting. Through process discussions, variations in trust and commitment can be normalized and even supported. To discuss trust, the leader may say, "I do not expect all of you to trust or commit at the same level. As a matter of fact, group is more interesting if there is variation." Unmet expectations should also be processed regularly by saying, "Is our group meeting your expectations? Is it helping?" If the answer is consistently "no," the leader must encourage problem solving so that the dissatisfied members may receive more help.

Therapist as Messenger

The leader should show respect for all members, including members who choose to leave the group. Discussions about the pros and cons of leaving should be objective and respectful, and should reinforce a member's right to choose to leave.

Education regarding lack of control in relationships, giving and receiving in relationships, betrayal, loss, and issues regarding shame and guilt may also be helpful. When a member leaves prematurely, the others must acknowledge their lack of control over other people's choices.

Therapist as Member

Whatever the reason, a member dropping out indicates a failure for her and perhaps for the group as a whole (Yalom, 1985). The leader may bear some responsibility. Perhaps the leader reinforced a scapegoat pattern, ignored the member's unique needs, or did not confront poor attendance. The leader should objectively explore the situation but refrain from destructive self-blame. Instead, the leader should devise plans so future dropouts can be prevented. Because of the leader's disappointment or anger, she or he may be tempted to make disparaging comments about a member sho dropped out, to the remaining members. These types of remarks should be limited to the leader's support network, where negative thoughts and feelings can be appropriately addressed and resolved.

❏ Individual Member Issues

SELF-DESTRUCTIVE BEHAVIORS

In one group of seven, five were experiencing severe depression. Two of those members had engaged in self-destructive behaviors including suicide attempts and self-mutilation. During one session, Tina related that the stress she experienced in the previous group precipitated some self-mutilating behavior. Upon hearing this, members were very distressed and some felt guilty for "causing" her to hurt herself. When another member, Donna, later shared her suicidal thoughts, the group refrained from any comment. They feared that their comments would somehow cause her to carry out her suicide plans. The leader then took a more directive role whenever a member displayed serious signs of self-destructive behavior.

Therapist as Monitor and Mediator

As indicated in chapter 1, various self-destructive behaviors are associated with past sexual abuse. As group therapists, we require that self-destructive members be seen by an individual therapist who will thoroughly address their behaviors. Because suicidal members have an individual therapist, the group should not be the member's lifeline. Discussion of a member's self-destructive threats and/or behavior should also be limited to protect the integrity of the group as a whole. Group rules regarding members' discussions of suicide and other self-destructive behaviors should be devised. Most groups decide that plans regarding suicide or other self-destructive behaviors should be discussed during individual therapy. Therefore, the members' discussions of lethality should be limited by the leader asking the suicidal member to contact her individual therapist. If the suicidal member refuses to contact her individual therapist, the member should be asked to remain in the room after group. At that time, the group therapist can either contact the individual therapist or arrange for appropriate intervention. Even though the individual therapist may be the primary lifeline, the group therapist should be able to analyze the lethality of suicidal threats and should be familiar with appropriate action plans.

In rare instances, a member may come to group after taking an overdose, injuring herself, or experiencing some similar emergency. Immediate intervention is then warranted. These interventions are one of the instances when a group therapist may act like an individual therapist. When safety is assured, the therapist can return to her group therapy role. The leader should then ask the group, "What are your reactions to what you just observed?" Most often other members will express relief that the leader has taken over and they are not responsible. At other times, however, members may have different reactions—especially if they mistrust the leader's interventions. For example, Betty had a long history of acting in a manipulative manner regarding her propensity toward suicide. During one group, when Betty mentioned her suicidal thoughts and attempts, the leader determined that immediate intervention was not warranted and Betty's individual therapist did not need immediate notification. The leader encouraged the group to go on with other discussions. Members later revealed their doubts about the leader's intervention. They had felt that Betty should have been hospitalized so they could feel assured about her safety. The leader then encouraged further discussion, during which she educated the group about the legal limitations regarding involuntary hospitalizations.

When self-destructive members are present, the issue of inter-member trust is especially pertinent. If others cannot trust that a member is committed to live, it is difficult to trust that member's commitment to the group. When members continually indicate they want to die, the group may need to accept that deep trust will not be possible. Being aware of and discussing self-destructive urges may awaken self-destructive thoughts and urges for all members. Members who were able to trust themselves to maintain personal safety may again struggle with their own suicidal potential.

Discussions of suicide introduce issues regarding responsibility. Members who are, or have been, close to someone self-destructive can provide helpful feedback to suicidal members about the ramifications of their actions. After Donna discussed her suicidal urges, Sue angrily recounted the many times her father attempted suicide. This angry interchange forced Donna to assess the potential effects of her self-destructiveness on her own children. Unlike Sue, many members are hesitant to respond to a suicidal member because of their concern that they may say something that would push the member to commit suicide. Members should not be held accountable when other's self-destructive behavior occurs subsequent to a discussion.

Although group rules limit members' discussion regarding the assessments of lethality, members are free to discuss the implications of suicide and self-injurious behavior. Members may help each other understand how their self-destructive behavior is a way to express self-hatred (Ganzarain & Buchele, 1987) or a way to relieve emotional distress. They may also discuss suicide from various philosophical or spiritual perspectives. Group members must ponder questions such as "Do people have a right to terminate their own lives?"; "What happens after death?"; and "Who is responsible if someone does commit suicide?" As these questions are discussed, members should develop their own viewpoints about these life and death issues. As they explore the meaning of their lives, members can clarify beliefs about their worthiness and entitlement to live.

Therapist as Messenger

The leader's responses should model that she or he will intervene to ensure a member's safety. When the leader decisively intervenes, members observe that individuals can maintain objectivity in the midst of emotional crises. They may also realize that power can be asserted and members' personal rights can still be respected. After observing the leader's reactions, members should be able to respond more directly to another's self-destructive verbalizations.

These types of groups may need to take many education breaks to discuss ethical, philosophical, and spiritual issues. A thorough review of commitment laws may be helpful in informing members of their personal rights and the leader's responsibilities and limitations. Education about the dynamics of suicidal thoughts and feelings is also helpful. The group could review reasons for living, such as survival and coping beliefs, responsibility to family, child-related concerns, fear of suicide, social disapproval, and moral objections (Linehan, Goodstein, Nielsen, & Chiles, 1983). Members may also explore reasons to live by discussing parts of self and how these parts work for or against the person as a whole.

Therapist as Member

Before the therapist commits to leading such a group, she or he must feel confident in her or his skills about handling suicidal behavior and must understand professional liability and ethical responsibility. Even if the leader is confident in her or his skills, the leader may feel anxious about self-destructive members. There are many judgments to be made and plans to be enacted. The leader's therapy team or supervisor, as well as other therapists working with the self-destructive members, should be consulted often.

POST-TRAUMATIC STRESS DISORDER

> In one group, five of seven members were experiencing intense symptoms of post-traumatic stress disorder (PTSD). It was not unusual for one or more members to have flashbacks during the group. Carla would often leave the room running from her brothers and Sara would "leave" by dissociating for long periods of time. Often members were numb to any emotional reactions. Because each group session felt like a crisis, members began to wonder if the group was helping or hurting.

Therapist as Monitor and Mediator

Many incest survivors experience symptoms of PTSD (see chapter 1). The theory of PTSD posits that stress related to past trauma that has been repressed will exert internal pressure until some resolution is accomplished (Horowitz, 1976). Because past incest is the focus of these groups, traumatic memories and related emotional reactions are often triggered by group interactions (Courtois, 1992). Some members may experience flashbacks and speak and act as if an abusive incident is presently occurring. For example, a member may scream, "Daddy, you're hurting me" or may appear to be experiencing physical pain. These flashbacks may be distressing to witness, and members often depend on the leader to react. The leader may ground the member having the flashback by orienting her to the present (Blake-White & Kline, 1985). For example, the leader may say, gently and firmly, "You're in group now, you are not with your daddy. You are having a flashback, your daddy is not here. Open your eyes and look at your hands, feel the arm of the chair, and look at me. You're grown now, the abuse isn't happening." If a member physically leaves the therapy room while in a flashback, the leader or another therapist should attend to that member. After the member returns and is reoriented, that member and the group will need to process. The leader may ask the member who was having the flashback, "How do you think this flashback will affect you later?"; "How do you feel about having the flashback in group?"?; "How can the group help you?"; or "What is this flashback trying to get you to realize?" Questions like these encourage that member to look beyond the memories to the beliefs and emotions associated with them. Group members can be asked, "What was it like for you to watch?" or "What did it trigger for you?"

At times, members do not have flashbacks but instead dissociate from the interaction (Blake-White & Kline, 1985; Braun, 1989; Chu & Dill, 1990). Members may appear to "space out" and be unable to respond to the interactions within the room. Once again, when a member dissociates, the therapist usually should attempt to reorient her. If the member is nonresponsive, the leader may enact a process discussion with the other members until the dissociative member responds. It is helpful for the group to have devised rules for coping with dissociative members so members will know how to react in a helpful way. Some who dissociate prefer to be brought out of the dissociative state, while others wish to be left alone until they come out themselves.

If a member reports concerns about new memories, those memories should be thoroughly explored in individual sessions. Using the group for the actual memory work may take a significant amount of group time and may seem like individual therapy with an audience. After individual work in which these memories have been explored and emotional issues have been addressed, the member may choose to share enough of the memory (i.e., age, who is involved, aftereffects) with the group so she can feel validated and understood. When memory work is done in group, or when memories are shared in detail, others tend to compare the content of their abuse with the content of others' abuse. Researchers have not determined the relationship of the content of the abuse with symptomatology (Finkelhor & Browne, 1985). Therefore, members should be assured that they have the right to experience their reactions regardless of the content of their abuse even if they perceive their abuse as "less invasive" than that of others.

It may be helpful to describe PTSD symptoms as, "Your mind's way of telling you it is time to work through the abuse." If members can trust that the symptoms are helpful to their recovery, they may be less frightened of them and willing to work with them and not against them. The members can then be encouraged to address the cognitive, emotional, and behavioral aspects of the memories so resolution can finally occur. The leader may share an analogy such as "It may feel like you are in the middle of a remodeling project. When you remodel a house, the process may feel distressful, but you can make desirable changes. Remember, the remodeled house will be more comfortable when the project is complete." Members who are experiencing active PTSD symptoms may be very receptive to adopting new beliefs that will eventually allow them to construct a "more comfortable" self-concept.

Therapist as Messenger

When the leader intervenes regarding PTSD symptoms and does not panic, she or he provides modeling. If members clearly see that the leader reacts calmly and confidently, they can relax and allow the leader to perform these functions. They can then learn how to respond helpfully to each other or themselves when such symptoms occur.

It may be helpful for the leader to review specific methods for addressing PTSD. Cole and Barney's (1987) concept of the "therapeutic window" may be especially helpful. The therapeutic window describes a model for addressing issues between the extremes of denial and intrusiveness. Also, information about crisis intervention, coping with stress, and dissociative reactions may be helpful. During these kinds of discussions, members may be utilized as "teaching assistants" by encouraging them to use their symptoms to illustrate the material being discussed.

Therapist as Member

The drama of watching a member go through flashbacks can be as frightening for the leader as it is for the group. The leader must have confidence that she or he can handle such interactions both personally and therapeutically, but must also be willing to ask for help when she or he does not have the necessary confidence. Many therapists, especially those new to this work, may feel emotionally overwhelmed when observing flashbacks. The leader needs a place where she or he can "dump" negative thoughts and feelings and still feel affirmed and emotionally supported.

Bobbie, an alcoholic, admitted during her third group meeting that she was "high." Just before the meeting, she had been at a bar and had had two drinks. Other members, especially those who had difficulty with their own or others' chemical dependency, were frightened and angry. One member was particularly upset because her perpetrator was an alcoholic who "blamed the abuse on the alcohol." Concerns about confidentiality were also expressed and members understandably asked, "How can we say anything in here and trust that Bobbie will be able to keep it confidential?" The leader intervened by asking Bobbie to leave the group meeting and requested that she schedule a session with her individual therapist within the week. Before returning to group, Bobbie had to assure members and the leader about her plans for sobriety and commitment to the group.

Therapist as Monitor and Mediator

Symptoms associated with concurrent diagnoses, such as chemical dependency, can be problematic for incest therapy groups. Addictions, personality disorders, depression, dissociative disorders, and PTSD are examples of common concurrent diagnoses (see chapter 1). Because substance use may have a direct impact on the functioning of the group, this section highlights symptoms related to chemical dependency.

Incest therapy is especially challenging for addicted members (Root, 1989). A waiting period after addiction treatment may be advised, especially if the member has continued difficulty with maintaining sobriety. Chemically dependent members who attend an incest therapy group should be informed of the clear prohibition against the use of addictive substances. Because it is not unusual for these members to relapse early in incest treatment, they may need to structure extra support for the first months of therapy. The general rule of no secrets is especially applicable. Because secrecy may enable the person to continue with addictive behaviors, all members must agree to "blow the whistle" if they are aware of addictive behaviors that members are not sharing with the group. If relapse does occur, the therapist and the group need to assess whether or not the relapse warrants the member's expulsion.

When working with this and other concurrent diagnoses, it is generally advisable that the addictive member get additional supportive treatment elsewhere. Although incest therapy groups address a variety of issues, the primary focus is on power, goodness, and importance as they relate to incest. Members with concurrent diagnoses likely need more attention regarding specific symptoms related to their diagnoses than can be provided in incest group therapy. Therapists in other treatment settings should agree to work as a team with the incest group therapist so all can be assured that pertinent issues are being addressed.

It may be advisable for members with certain diagnoses to educate the group regarding symptoms of their disorder. For example, a manic-depressive member was noticeably different during her manic phase. Because she had previously educated the group about behaviors that may occur during a manic episode, group members stayed connected with her despite her symptomatic behavior. Likewise, members with multiple personality disorder (MPD) may inform members about speech and mannerisms associated with different personalities. (We advise that those clearly diagnosed with MPD not be included in group until they have an understanding of their intrapsychic structure. We also advise that they be actively involved in individual therapy.)

As members discuss their concurrent diagnoses, they can begin to assess the relationship of these diagnoses to the incest experience. As a result, some may reassess the behaviors associated with their diagnosis as maladaptive coping strategies or developmental responses to childhood trauma (Briere, 1989; Summit, 1983). Those who may have previously identified themselves as insane, crazy, or stupid may now identify themselves as having symptoms related to the past stress of the abuse.

Therapist as Messenger

It is important that the leader not enable addictive processes or other symptoms related to a concurrent diagnosis. Clear boundaries are required not only with the symptomatic member but also with other treatment professionals. The group therapist should be clear about which issues should be addressed in which setting, and maintain that clarity.

An education break may be needed to lecture specifically about various diagnoses and associated symptoms. The group can be referred to specific reading material when applicable.

Therapist as Member

Working with multiply diagnosed members may be challenging. The leader may need to learn more about specific diagnoses and treatment regimens to understand how certain members may react in group. If the leader has the same or similar diagnosis as members in the group (e.g., chemical dependency), she or he may unconsciously act out personal issues within the group. Again we advise that the leader use a support network. In some cases the leader may need to engage the services of a personal therapist.

❏ Final Thoughts

It is not possible to work in this field of clinical practice without becoming acutely aware of the need for well-designed and executed treatment outcome studies. A large body of research addresses the consequences of incestuous abuse; this is only beginning to clarify complex patterns and interactions associated with abuse and its sequelae. Very few well-controlled studies address the effectiveness of programs and techniques or the applicability of particular treatment strategies to certain types of experiences. We have attempted to function as researchers as well as clinicians (Donaldson & Edwards, 1988; Edwards & Donaldson, 1989), but find that we have insufficient time to design the kinds of research protocols needed to complete comprehensive clinical research.

It is our hope that the concepts presented in this book will assist the practitioner in better serving adult incest survivors and also provide some organization and material for future clinical research. Because this is a relatively new area of treatment, we and all practitioners must accept the challenge to continue to adapt accepted approaches. Moreover, we must develop and empirically test new and revised treatment modalities in order to assure that the best possible programs will be available for this population.

References

Abney, V., Yang, J., & Paulson, M. (1992). Transference issues unique to long-term group psychotherapy of adult women molested as children. *Journal of Interpersonal Violence, 7*(4), 559-569.

Alexander, P. C. (1985). A systems theory conceptualization of incest. *Family Process, 24,* 79-88.

Alexander, P. C. (1992a). Application of attachment theory to the study of sexual abuse. *Journal of Consulting and Clinical Psychology, 60*(2), 185-195.

Alexander, P. C. (1992b). Introduction to the special section on adult survivors of childhood sexual abuse. *Journal of Consulting and Clinical Psychology, 60*(2), 165-166.

Alexander, P. C., Neimeyer, R. A., Follette, V. M., Moore, M. K., & Harter, S. (1989). A comparison of group treatments of women sexually abused. *Journal of Consulting and Clinical Psychology, 57*(4), 479-483.

Alexander, P. C., Neimeyer, R. A., & Follette, V. M. (1991). Group therapy for women sexually abused as children: A controlled study and investigation of individual differences. *Journal of Interpersonal Violence, 6*(2), 218-231.

Allers, C. T., Benjack, K. J., & Allers, N. T. (1992). Unresolved childhood sexual abuse: Are older adults affected? *Journal of Counseling and Development, 71*(1), 14-17.

Alter-Reid, K., Gibbs, M. S., Lachenmeyer, J. R., Sigal, J., & Masseth, N. A. (1986). Sexual abuse of children: A review of the empirical findings. *Clinical Psychology Review, 6,* 249-266.

American Psychiatric Association. (1980). *Diagnostic and statistical manual of mental disorders* (3rd ed.). Washington, DC: APA.

154

Apolinsky, S. R., & Wilcoxon, S. A. (1991). Symbolic confrontation with women survivors of childhood sexual victimization. *Journal for Specialists in Group Work, 16*(2), 85-90.

Armsworth, M. W. (1989). Therapy of incest survivors: Abuse or support? *Child Abuse & Neglect, 13,* 549-562.

Axelroth, E. (1991). Retrospective incest group therapy for university women. *Journal of College Student Psychotherapy, 5*(2), 81-100.

Barnard, C. P., & Hirsch, C. (1985). Borderline personality and victims of incest. *Psychological Reports, 57,* 715-718.

Beck, A. T. (1976). *Cognitive therapy and the emotional disorder.* New York: International Universities Press.

Beck, A. T. (1978). *Beck depression inventory* (rev. ed.). Philadelphia: Center for Cognitive Therapy

Becker, J. V., Skinner, L. J., Abel, G. C., & Cichon, J. (1986). Level of post-assault sexual functioning in rape and incest victims. *Archives of Sexual Behavior, 15*(1), 37-49.

Beckman, K. A., & Burns, G. L. (1990). Relations of sexual abuse and bulimia in college women. *International Journal of Eating Disorders, 9*(5), 487-492.

Bergart, A. M. (1986, May). Isolation to intimacy: Incest survivors in group therapy. *Social Casework: The Journal of Contemporary Social Work,* 266-275.

Beutler, L. E., & Hill, C. E. (1992). Process and outcomes research in the treatment of adult victims of childhood sexual abuse: Methodological issues. *Journal of Consulting and Clinical Psychology, 60*(2), 204-212.

Blake-White, J., & Kline, C. M. (1985, September). Treating the dissociative process in adult victims of childhood incest. *Social Casework: The Journal of Contemporary Social Work,* 394-402.

Bonney, W. C., Randall, D. A., & Cleveland, J. D. (1986). An analysis of client-perceived curative factors in a therapy group of former incest victims. *Small Group Behavior, 17*(3), 303-321.

Brandt, L. (1989). A short-term group therapy model for treatment of adult female survivors of childhood incest. *Group, 13*(2), 74-82.

Braun, B. G. (1989). Psychotherapy of the survivor of incest with a dissociative disorder. *Psychiatric Clinics of North America, 12*(2), 307-324.

Brickman, J. (1984). Feminist, nonsexist, and traditional models of therapy: Implications for working with incest. *Women & Therapy, 3*(1), 49-67.

Briere, J. N. (1988). Controlling for family variables in abuse effects research: A critique of the "partialing" approach. *Journal of Interpersonal Violence, 3*(1), 80-89.

Briere, J. N. (1989). *Therapy for adults molested as children: Beyond survival.* New York: Springer.

Briere, J. N. (1992a). *Child abuse trauma: Theory and treatment of the lasting effects.* Newbury Park, CA: Sage.

Briere, J. N. (1992b). Methodological issues in the study of sexual abuse effects. *Journal of Consulting and Clinical Psychology, 60*(2), 196-203.

Briere, J. N., Evans, D., Runtz, M., & Wall, T. (1988). Symptomatology in men who were molested as children: A comparison study. *American Journal of Orthopsychiatry, 58*(3), 457-461.

Briere J. N., & Runtz, M. (1986). Suicidal thoughts and behaviours in former sexual abuse victims. *Canadian Journal of Behavioural Science, 18,* 413-423.

Briere J. N., & Runtz, M. (1987). Post sexual abuse trauma: Data and implications for clinical practice. *Journal of Interpersonal Violence, 2*(4), 367-379.

Briere, J. N., & Runtz, M. (1988a). Symptomatology associated with childhood sexual victimization in a nonclinical adult sample. *Child Abuse & Neglect, 12*, 51-59.

Briere, J. N., & Runtz, M. (1988b). Research with adults molested as children. In G. E. Wyatt & G. J. Powell (Eds.), *Lasting effects of child sexual abuse*, 85-100. Newbury Park, CA: Sage.

Briere, J. N., & Runtz, M. (1989). University males' sexual intrest in predicting potential indices of pedophilia in a nonforensic sample. *Child Abuse and Neglect, 13*, 65-75.

Briere, J. N., & Runtz, M. (1990). Differential adult symptomatology associated with three types of child abuse histories. *Child Abuse and Neglect, 14*, 357-364.

Brittain, D., & Merriam, K. (1988). Groups for significant others of survivors of child sexual abuse. *Journal of Interpersonal Violence, 3*(1), 90-101.

Brown, G. R., & Anderson, B. (1991). Psychiatric morbidity in adult inpatients with childhood histories of sexual and physical abuse. *American Journal of Psychiatry, 148*(1), 55-61.

Browne, A., & Finkelhor, D. (1986). Impact of child sexual abuse: A review of the research. *Psychological Bulletin, 99*, 66-77.

Bryer, J. B., Nelson, B. A., Miller, J. B., & Krol, P. A. (1987). Childhood sexual and physical abuse as factors in adult psychiatric illness. *American Journal of Psychiatry, 144*(11), 1426-1430.

Budman, S. H., Soldz, S., Demby, A., Feldstein, M., Springer, T., & Davis, M. (1989). Cohesion, alliance and outcome in group psychotherapy. *Psychiatry, 52*, 339-350.

Bulik, C., Sullivan, P., & Rorty, M. (1989). Childhood sexual abuse in women with bulimia. *Journal of Clinical Psychiatry, 50*, 460-464.

Bushnell, J. A., Wells, J. E., & Oakley-Browne, M. A. (1992). Long-term effects of intrafamilial sexual abuse in childhood. *Acta Psychiatrica Scandinavica, 85*, 136-142.

Cahill, C., Llewelyn, S. P., & Pearson, C. (1991). Treatment of sexual abuse that occurred in childhood: A review. *British Journal of Clinical Psychology, 30*(1), 1-12.

Calam, R. M., & Slade, P. D. (1989). Sexual experience and eating problems in female undergraduates. *International Journal of Eating Disorders, 8*(4), 391-397.

Carroll, J., Schaffer, C., Spensley, J., & Abramowitz, S. (1980). Family experiences of self-mutilating patients. *American Journal of Psychiatry, 137*, 852-853.

Carver, C. M., Stalker, C., Stewart, E., & Abraham, B. (1989). The impact of group therapy for adult survivors of childhood sexual abuse. *Canadian Journal of Psychiatry, 34*(8), 753-758.

Celano, M. (1992). A developmental model of victims' internal attributions of responsibility for sexual abuse. *Journal of Interpersonal Violence, 7*(1), 57-69.

Chu, J. A., & Dill, D. L. (1990). Dissociative symptoms in relation to childhood physical and sexual abuse. *American Journal of Psychiatry, 147*(7), 887-892.

Cohen, L. J. (1988). Providing treatment and support for partners of sexual-assault survivors. *Psychotherapy, 25*, 94-98.

Coker, L. S. (1990). A therapeutic recovery model for the female adult incest survivor. *Issues in Mental Health Nursing, 11*, 109-123.

Cole, C. H., & Barney, E. E. (1987). Safeguards and the therapeutic window: A group treatment strategy for adult incest survivors. *American Journal of Orthopsychiatry, 57*(4), 601-609.

Cole, C. L. (1985). A group design for adult female survivors of childhood incest. *Women and Therapy, 4*(3), 71-82.

Cole, P. M., & Putnam, F. W. (1992). Effect of incest on self and social functioning: A developmental psychopathology perspective. *Journal of Consulting and Clinical Psychology, 60*(2), 174-184.

Connors, M. E., & Morse, W. (1993). Sexual abuse and eating disorders: A review. *International Journal of Eating Disorders, 13*(1), 1-11.

Conte, J., & Schuerman, J. R. (1987). Factors associated with an increased impact of child sexual abuse. *Child Abuse & Neglect, 11*, 201-211.

Coons, P. M., Bowman, E. S., Pellow, T. A., & Schneider, P. (1989). Post-traumatic aspects of the treatment of victims of sexual abuse and incest. *Psychiatric Clinics of North America, 12*(2), 325-335.

Coons, P. M., & Milstein, V. (1986). Psychosexual disturbances in multiple personality: Characteristics, etiology, and treatment. *Journal of Clinical Psychiatry, 47*(3), 106-110.

Corey, G. (1985). *Theory and practice of group counseling* (2nd ed.). Pacific Grove, CA: Brooks/Cole.

Courtois, C. A. (1988). *Healing the incest wound: Adult survivors in therapy.* New York: Norton.

Courtois, C. A. (1992). The memory retrieval process in incest survivor therapy. *Journal of Child Sexual Abuse, 1*(1), 15-31.

Courtois, C. A., & Leehan, J. (1982). Group treatment for grown-up abused children. *Personnel and Guidance Journal, 60*, 564-566.

Courtois, C. A., & Watts, D. C. (1982). Counseling adult women who experienced incest in childhood or adolescence. *The Personnel and Guidance Journal, 60*, 275-279

Cunningham, J., Pearce, R., & Pearce, P. (1988). Childhood sexual abuse and medical complaints in adult women. *Journal of Interpersonal Violence, 3*(2), 131-144.

Deighton, J., & McPeek, P. (1985, September). Group treatment: Adult victims of childhood sexual abuse. *Social Casework: The Journal of Contemporary Social Work,* 403-410.

Delvey, J. Jr. (1982). Parenting errors and their correction in group psychotherapy. *American Journal of Psychotherapy, 36*, 523-535.

de Young, M. (1982). Self-injurious behavior in incest victims: A research note. *Child Welfare, 61*(8), 577-584.

Dimock, P. T. (1988). Adult males sexually abused as children: Characteristics and implications for treatment. *Journal of Interpersonal Violence, 3*(2), 203-221.

Donaldson, M. A. (1983). *Incest years after: Putting the pain to rest.* Fargo, ND: The Village Family Service Center.

Donaldson, M. A. (1986). *Incest years after: A lecture on theory and treatment.* Fargo, ND: The Village Family Service Center.

Donaldson, M. A. (1988). *Memory work: Individual therapy with adult incest survivors.* Fargo, ND: The Village Family Service Center.

Donaldson, M. A., & Edwards, P. (1988, November). *Responses to childhood incest: A questionnaire for clinical use.* Paper presented at the annual meeting of the National Association of Social Workers, Philadelphia, PA.

Donaldson, M. A., & Gardner. R. (1985). Diagnosis and treatment of traumatic stress among women after childhood incest. In C. R. Figley (Ed.), *Trauma and its wake: The study and treatment of post-traumatic stress disorder* (pp. 356-377). New York: Brunner/Mazel.

Donaldson, M. A., & Cordes-Green, S. (1987). *Incest, years after: Learning to cope successfully.* Fargo, ND: The Village Family Service Center.

Douglas, A. R., & Matson, I. C., (1989). An account of a time-limited therapeutic group in an NHS setting for women with a history of incest. *Group, 13*(2), 83-94.

Douglas, A. R., Matson, I. C., & Hunter, S. (1989). Sex therapy for women incestuously abused as children. *Sexual and Marital Therapy, 4*(2), 143-159.

Draucker, C. B. (1989). Cognitive adaptation of female incest survivors. *Journal of Consulting and Clinical Psychology, 57*(5), 668-670.

Drews, J., & Bradley, R. (1989). Group treatment for adults molested as children: An educational and therapeutic approach. *Social Work with Groups, 12*(3), 57-75.

Drossman, D., Lesuman, J., Nachman, G., Zhiming, L., Gluck, H., Toomey, T., & Mitchell, C. (1990). Sexual and physical abuse in women with functional or organic gastrointestinal disorders. *International Journal of Medicine, 113,* 828-833.

Edwards, J., & Alexander, P. (1992). The contribution of family background to the long-term adjustment of women sexually abused as children. *Journal of Interpersonal Violence, 7*(3), 306-320.

Edwards, P., & Donaldson, M. A. (1989). Assessment of symptoms in adult survivors of incest: A factor analytic study of the responses to childhood incest questionnaire. *Child Abuse & Neglect, 13,* 101-110.

Finkelhor, D. (1979). *Sexually victimized children.* New York: Free Press.

Finkelhor, D. (1984). *Child sexual abuse: New theory & research.* New York: Free Press.

Finkelhor, D. (1987). The sexual abuse of children: Current research reviewed. *Psychiatric Annals, 17*(4), 233-239.

Finkelhor, D., (1990). Early and long-term effects of child sexual abuse: An update. *Professional Psychology: Research and Practice, 21*(5), 325-330.

Finkelhor, D., & Browne, A. (1985). The traumatic impact of child sexual abuse: A conceptualization. *American Journal of Orthopsychiatry, 55*(4), 530-541.

Finkelhor, D., Hotaling, G., Lewis, I. A., & Smith, C. (1989). Sexual abuse and its relationship to later sexual satisfaction, marital status, religion, and attitudes. *Journal of Interpersonal Violence, 4*(4), 379-399.

Finkelhor, D., Hotaling, G., Lewis, I. A., & Smith, C. (1990). Sexual abuse in a national survey of adult men and women: Prevalence, characteristics, and risk factors. *Child Abuse & Neglect, 14,* 19-28.

Finn, S. E., Hartman, M., Leon, G. R., & Lawson, L. (1986). Eating disorders and sexual abuse: Lack of confirmation for a clinical hypothesis. *International Journal of Eating Disorders, 5*(6), 1051-1060.

Fisher, S. (1985). Identity of two: The phenomenology of shame in borderline development and treatment. *Psychotherapy Theory, Research & Practice, 22*(1), 101-109.

Follette, V. M., Alexander, P. C., & Follette, W. C. (1991). Individual predictors of outcome in group treatment for incest survivors. *Journal of Consulting and Clinical Psychology, 59*(1), 150-155.

Fossum, M. A., & Mason, M. J. (1986). *Facing shame: Families in recovery.* New York: Norton.

Forward, S., & Buck, C. (1978). *Betrayal of innocence: Incest and its devastation.* Los Angeles: J. P. Tarcher.

Fowler, C., Burns, S. R., & Roehl, J. E. (1983). The role of group therapy in incest counseling. *International Journal of Family Therapy, 5*(2), 127-135.

Ganzarain, R., & Buchele, B. (1987). Acting out during group psychotherapy for incest. *International Journal of Group Psychotherapy, 37*(2), 185-200.

Garmezy, N. (1983). Stressors of childhood. In N. Garmezy and M. Rutter (Eds.), *Stress, coping, and development in children* (pp. 43-84). New York: McGraw-Hill.

Gelinas, D. (1983). The persisting negative effects of incest. *Psychiatry, 46,* 312-332.

Giaretto, H. (1981). A comprehensive child sexual abuse treatment program. In P. Mrazek & C. Kempe (Eds.), *Sexually abused children and their families* (pp. 179-198). New York: Pergamon.

Gilligan, S. G., & Kennedy, C. M. (1989). Solutions and resolutions: Erickson's hypnotherapy with incest survivor groups. *Journal and Systemic Therapies, 8*(4), 9-17.

Gold, E. R. (1986). Long-term effects of sexual victimization in childhood: An attributional approach. *Journal of Consulting and Clinical Psychology, 54*(4), 471-475.

Goodman, B., & Nowak-Scibelli, E. (1985). Group treatment for women incestuously abused as children. *International Journal of Group Psychotherapy, 35,* 531-544.

Goodwin, J. M., Cheeves, K., & Connell, V. (1990). Borderline and other severe symptoms in adult survivors of incestuous abuse. *Psychiatric Annals, 20*(1), 22-31.

Gordy, P. L. (1983). Group work that supports adult victims of childhood incest. *Social Casework, 64*(5), 300-307.

Greenwald, E., & Leitenberg, H. (1990). Posttraumatic stress disorder in a nonclinical and nonstudent sample of adult women sexually abused as children. *Journal of Interpersonal Violence, 5*(2), 217-228.

Gross, R. J., Doerr, H., Caldirola, D., Guzinski, G., & Ripley, H. (1980-1981). Borderline syndrome and incest in chronic pelvic pain patients. *International Journal Psychiatry in Medicine, 10*(1), 79-96.

Grove, D. J., & Panzer, B. I. (1989). *Resolving traumatic memories: Metaphors and symbols in psychotherapy.* New York: Irvington Publishers, Inc.

Hall, R., Kassees, J., & Hoffman, C. (1986). Treatment for survivors of incest. *Journal for Specialists in Group Work, 11*(2), 85-92.

Hall, R. C., Tice, L., Beresford, R. P., Wooley, B., & Hall, A. K. (1989). Sexual abuse in patients with anorexia nervosa and bulimia. *Psychosomatics, 30*(1), 73-79.

Harter, S., Alexander, P. C., & Neimeyer, R. A. (1988). Long-term effects of incestuous child abuse in college women: Social adjustment, social cognition, and family characteristics. *Journal of Consulting and Clinical Psychology, 56,* 5-8.

Hays, K. F. (1985). Electra in mourning: Grief work and the adult incest survivor. In E. M. Stern (Ed.), *Psychotherapy and the grieving patient* (pp. 45-58). New York: Haworth.

Hays, K. F. (1987). The conspiracy of silence revisited: Group therapy with adult survivors of incest. *Journal G. P. P. S.,* Winter, 143-156.

Herman, J. L. (1981). *Father-daughter incest.* Cambridge: Harvard University Press.

Herman, J. L., Perry, J. C., & van der Kolk, B. A. (1989). Childhood trauma in borderline personality disorder. *American Journal of Psychiatry, 146,* 490-495.

Herman, J. L., Russell, D., & Trocki, K. (1986). Long-tern effects of incestuous abuse in childhood. *American Journal of Psychiatry, 143* (10), 1293-1296.

Herman, J. L., & Schatzow, E. (1984). Time-limited group therapy for women with a history of incest. *International Journal of Group Psychotherapy,* 605-616.

Herman, J. L., & Schatzow, E. (1987). Recovery and verification of memories of childhood sexual trauma. *Psychoanalytic Psychology, 4,* 1-14.

Horowitz, M. J. (1976). *Stress Response Syndromes.* New York: Jason Aronson.

Hunter, J. A. (1991). A comparison of the psychosocial maladjustment of adult males and females sexually molested as children. *Journal of Interpersonal Violence, 6*(2), 205-217.

Hurley, D. L. (1990). Incest and the development of alcoholism in adult female survivors. *Alcoholism Treatment Quarterly, 7*(2), 41-56.

Jackson, J., Calhoun, K., Amick, A., Maddever, H., & Habif, V. (1990). Young adult women who report childhood intrafamilial sexual abuse: Subsequent adjustment. *Archives of Sexual Behavior, 19*(3), 211-221.

Jacobson, A., & Herald, D. (1990). The relevance of childhood sexual abuse to adult psychiatric inpatient care. *Hospital and Community Psychiatry, 41*(2), 154-158.

Jehu, D. (1988). *Beyond sexual abuse: Therapy with women who were childhood victims.* Chichester, UK: Wiley.

Kaplan, M., Becker, J., & Tenke, C. (1991). Influence of abuse history on male adolescent self-reported comfort with interviewer gender. *Journal of Interpersonal Violence, 6*(1), 3-11.

Kearney-Cooke, A. (1988). Group treatment of sexual abuse among women with eating disorders. *Women & Therapy, 7,* 5-21.

Kendall-Tackett, K. (1991). Characteristics of abuse that influence when adults molested as children seek treatment. *Journal of Interpersonal Violence, 6*(4), 486-493.

Kinzl, J., & Biebl, W. (1991). Sexual abuse of girls: Aspects of the genesis of mental disorders and therapeutic implications. *Acta Psychiatrica Scandinavica, 83,* 427-431.

Knight, C. (1990). Use of support groups with adult female survivors of child sexual abuse. *Social Work, 35*(3), 202-206.

Kriedler, M. C., & England, D. B. (1990). Empowerment through group support: Adult women who are survivors of incest. *Journal of Family Violence 5*(1), 35-42.

Kriedler, M. C., & Hassan, M. (1992). Use of an interactional model with survivors of incest. *Issues in Mental Health Nursing, 13,* 149-158.

Ladwig, G. B., & Anderson, M. D. (1989). Substance abuse in women: Relationship between chemical dependency in women and past reports of physical and sexual abuse. *International Journal of Addiction, 24,* 739-754.

Laube, J., & Wieland, V. (1990). Developing prescriptions to accelerate group process in incest and bulimia treatment. *Journal of Independent Social Work, 4*(2), 95-112.

Lehman, L. (1985). The relationship of depression to other *DSM-III* Axis I disorders. In E. Beckham & W. Leber (Eds.), *Handbook of depression: Treatment, assessment and research* (pp. 669-699). Homewood, IL: Dorsey Press.

Lindberg, F. H., & Distad, L. J. (1985). Post-traumatic stress disorders in women who experienced childhood incest. *Child Abuse & Neglect, 9,* 329-334.

Linehan, M., Goodstein, J., Nielsen, S., & Chiles, J. (1983). Reasons for staying alive when you are thinking of killing yourself: The reason for living inventory. *Journal of Consulting and Clinical Psychology, 51*(2), 276-286.

Loftus, E. F. (1993). The reality of repressed memories. *American Psychologist, 5* (48), 518-537.

Long, P., & Jackson, J. (1991). Children sexually abused by multiple perpetrators. *Journal of Interpersonal Violence, 6*(2), 147-159.

Lundberg-Love, P. K., Marmion, S., Ford, K., Geffner, R., & Peacock, L. (1992). The long-term consequences of childhood incestuous victimization upon adult women's psychological symptomatology. *Journal of Child Sexual Abuse, 1*(1), 81-102.

MacFarlane, K., & Korbin, J. (1983). Confronting the incest secret long after the fact: A family study of multiple victimization with strategies for intervention. *Child Abuse & Neglect, 7,* 225-240.

Madonna, P., Van Scoyk, S., & Jones, D. (1991). Family interactions with incest and nonincest families. *American Journal of Psychiatry, 148*(1), 46-49.

Maltz, W., & Holman, B. (1987). *Incest and sexuality: A guide to understanding and healing.* Lexington, MA: Lexington Books.

Mara, J. (1983). A lesbian perspective. *Women & Therapy, 2,* 145-155.

Marhoefer-Dvorak, S., Resick, P., Hutter, C., & Girelli, S. (1988). Single- versus multiple-incident rape victims: A comparison of psychological reactions to rape. *Journal of Interpersonal Violence, 3*(2), 145-160.

McBride, M., & Emerson, S. (1989). Group work with women who were molested as children. *Journal for Specialists in Group Work, 14*(1), 25-33.

McCann, I. L., & Pearlman, L. (1990). *Psychological trauma and the adult survivor: Theory, therapy, and transformation.* New York: Brunner/Mazel.

Meiselman, K. C. (1978). *Incest: A psychological study of cause and effects with treatment recommendations.* San Francisco: Jossey-Bass.

Meiselman, K. C. (1990). *Resolving the trauma of incest.* San Francisco: Jossey-Bass.

Miller, J., Moeller, D., Kaufman, A., DiVasto, P., Pathak, D., & Christy, J. (1978). Recidivism among sex assault victims. *American Journal of Psychiatry, 135,* 1103-1104.

Millon, T., & Kotik, D. (1985). The relationship of depression to disorders of personality. In E. Beckham & W. Leber (Eds.), *Handbook of depression: Treatment, assessment and research* (pp. 700-744). Homewood, IL: Dorsey Press.

Moore, J. M. (1986). Civil remedies for incest survivors. *Response, 9*(2), 11-15.

Murphy, S., Kilpatrick, D., Amick-McMullan, A., Veronen, L., Paduhovich, J., Best, C., Villeponteaux, L., & Saunders, B. (1988). Current psychological functioning of child sexual assault survivors: A community study. *Journal of Interpersonal Violence, 3*(1), 55-79.

Nigg, J., Silk, K., Westen, D., Lohr, N., Gold, L., Goodrich, S., & Ogata, S. (1991). Object representations in the early memories of sexually abused borderline patients. *American Journal of Psychiatry, 148*(7), 864-869.

O'Connell, M. A., Leberg, E., & Donaldson, C. R. (1990). *Working with sex offenders: Guidelines for therapist selection.* Newbury Park, CA: Sage.

Ogata, S. N., Silk, K. R., Goodrich, S., Lohr, N. E. Westen, D., & Hill, E. M. (1990). Childhood sexual and physical abuse in adult patients with borderline personality disorder. *American Journal of Psychiatry, 147,* 1008-1013.

O'Hare, J., & Taylor, K. (1983). The reality of incest. In J. Hamerman-Robins & R. Josefowitz-Siegel (Eds.), *Women changing therapy: New assessments, values, and strategies in feminist therapy* (pp. 215-229). New York: Haworth.

Oppenheimer, R., Howells, K., Palmer, R. L., & Chaloner, D. A. (1985). Adverse sexual experience in childhood and clinical eating disorders: A preliminary description. *Journal of Psychiatry Research, 19*(2/3), 357-361.

Palmer, R. L., & Oppenheimer, R. (1992). Childhood sexual experiences with adults: A comparison of women with eating disorders and those with other diagnoses. *International Journal of Eating Disorders, 12*(4), 359-364.

Parker, S., & Parker, H. (1991). Female victims of child sexual abuse: Adult adjustment. *Journal of Family Violence, 6*(2), 183-197.

Peters, S. D. (1988). Child sexual abuse and later psychological problems. In G. E. Wyatt & G. J. Powell (Eds.), *Lasting effects of child sexual abuse* (pp. 101-117). Newbury Park, CA: Sage.

Pope, H. G., & Hudson, J. I. (1992). Is childhood sexual abuse a risk factor for bulimia nervosa? *American Journal of Psychiatry, 149*(4), 455-463.

Pribor, D. F., & Dinwiddie, S. H. (1992). Psychiatric correlates of incest in childhood. *American Journal of Psychiatry, 149*(1), 52-56.

Putnam, F. W. (1989). *Diagnosis and treatment of multiple personality disorder*. New York: Guilford.

Putnam, F. W., Guroff, J. J., Silberman, E. K., Barban, L., & Post, R. M. (1986). The clinical phenomenology of multiple personality disorder: Review of 100 recent cases. *Journal of Clinical Psychiatry, 47*(6), 285-293.

Roberts, L., & Lie, G. (1989). A group therapy approach to the treatment of incest. *Social Work With Groups. 12*(3), 77-91.

Root, M. P. (1989). Treatment failures, the role of sexual victimization in women's addictive behavior. *American Journal of Orthopsychiatry, 59*(4), 542-549.

Root, M. P., & Fallon, P. (1988). The incidence of victimization experiences in a bulimic sample. *Journal of Interpersonal Violence, 3*(2), 161-173.

Root, M. P., & Fallon, P. (1989). Treating the victimized bulimic: The functions of binge-purge behavior. *Journal of Interpersonal Violence, 4*(1), 90-100.

Rose, S. R. (1989). Members leaving groups: Theoretical and practical considerations. *Small Group Behavior, 20*(4), 524-535.

Rosenfeld, A. A. (1979). Incidence of a history of incest among 18 female psychiatric patients. *American Journal of Psychiatry, 136*(6), 791-795.

Ross, C. A., Miller, S. D., Bjornson, L., Reagor, P., Fraser, G. A., & Anderson, G. (1991). Abuse histories in 102 cases of multiple personality disorder. *Canadian Journal of Psychiatry, 36*, 97-101.

Rowe, W., & Savage, S. (1988, May). Sex therapy with female incest survivors. *Social Casework: The Journal of Contemporary Social Work*, 265-271.

Russell, D. (1986). *The secret trauma: Incest in the lives of girls and women*. New York: Basic Books.

Russell, D., Schurman, R., & Trocki, K. (1988). Long-term effects of incestuous abuse: A comparison of Afro-American and white American victims. In G. E. Wyatt & G. J. Powell (Eds.), *Lasting effects of child sexual abuse* (pp. 119-134). Newbury Park, CA: Sage.

Saunders, B., Villeponteaux, L., Lipovsky, J., Kilpatrick, D., & Veronen, L. J. (1992). Child sexual assault as a risk factor for mental disorders among women. *Journal of Interpersonal Violence, 7*(2), 189-204.

Schaef, A. W. (1986). *Co-dependence: Misunderstood-mistreated*. San Francisco: Harper & Row.

Schulman, L. (1979). *The skill of helping individuals and groups*. Itasca, IL: F. E. Peacock.

Scott, R. L., & Stone, D. A. (1986). MMPI profile constellations in incest families. *Journal of Consulting and Clinical Psychology, 54*(3), 364-368.

Scott, R., & Thoner, G. (1986). Ego deficits in anorexia nervosa patients and incest victims: An MMPI comparative analysis. *Psychological Reports, 58*, 839-846.

Sedney, M. A., & Brooks, B. (1984). Factors associated with a history of childhood sexual experience in a nonclinical female population. *Journal of the American Academy of Child Psychiatry, 23*, 215-218.

Shapiro, S., (1987). Self-mutilation and self-blame in incest victims. *American Journal of Psychotherapy, 41*(1), 46-54.

Siegel, D., & Romig, C. (1988) Treatment of adult survivors of childhood sexual assault: Imagery within a systemic framework. *American Journal of Family Therapy, 16*(3), 229-242.

Silver, R., Boon, C., & Stones, M. H. (1983). Searching for meaning in misfortune: Making sense of incest. *Journal of Social Issues, 39*, 81-102.

Singer, K. I. (1989). Group work with men who experienced incest in childhood. *American Journal of Orthopsychiatry, 59*(3), 468-472.

Singer, M. I., Petchers, M. K., & Hussey, D. (1989). The relationship between sexual abuse and substance abuse among psychiatrically hospitalized patients. *Child Abuse and Neglect, 13,* 319-325.

Sloan, G., & Leichner, P. (1986). Is there a relationship between sexual abuse or incest and eating disorders? *Canadian Journal of Psychiatry, 31,* 656-660.

Smolak, L., Levine, M., & Sullens, E. (1990). Are child sexual experiences related to eating-disorders attitudes and behaviors in a college sample? *International Journal of Eating Disorders, 9*(2), 167-178.

Spielberger, C. M., Gorsuch, R. L., Lushene, R., Vagg, P. R., & Jacobs, G. A. (1968). *Self-evaluation questionnaire.* Palo Alto, CA: Consulting Psychologists Press.

Steiger, H., & Zanko, M. (1990). Sexual traumata among eating-disordered, psychiatric, and normal female groups: Comparison of prevalences and defense styles. *Journal of Interpersonal Violence, 5*(1), 74-86.

Stein, J. A., Golding, J. M., Siegel, J. M., Burnam, M. A., & Sorenson, S. B. (1988). Long-term psychological sequelae of child sexual abuse. In G. E. Wyatt & G. J. Powell (Eds.), *Lasting effects of child sexual abuse* (pp. 135-156). Newbury Park, CA: Sage.

Sullivan, E. (1988). Associations between chemical dependency and sexual problems in nurses. *Journal of Interpersonal Violence, 3*(3), 326-330.

Summit, R. C. (1983). The child sexual abuse accommodation syndrome. *Child Abuse & Neglect, 7,* 177-193.

Summit, R. C. (1988). Hidden victims, hidden pain: Societal Avoidance and sexual abuse. In G. E. Wyatt & G. J. Powell (Eds.), *Lasting effects of child sexual abuse* (pp. 39-60). Newbury Park, CA: Sage.

Swett, C., Cohen, C. Surrey, J., Compaine A., & Chavez, R. (1991). High rates of alcohol use and history of physical and sexual abuse among women outpatients. *American Journal of Drug and Alcohol Abuse, 17*(1), 49-60.

Swink, K. K., & Leveille, A. E. (1986). From victim to survivor: A new look at the issues and recovery process for adult incest survivors. In D. Howard (Ed.), *The dynamics of feminist therapy* (pp. 119-141). New York: Haworth.

Terr, L. C. (1991). Childhood traumas: An outline and overview. *American Journal of Psychiatry, 148*(1), 10-20.

Tsai, M., Feldman-Summers, S., & Edgar, M. (1979). Childhood molestation: Variables related to differential impacts on psychosexual functioning in adult women. *Journal of Abnormal Psychology, 88*(4), 401-417.

Tsai, M. M., & Wagner, N. N. (1978). Therapy groups for women sexually molested as children. *Archives of Sexual Behavior, 7*(5), 417-427.

Van Buskirk, S., & Cole. C. (1983). Characteristics of eight women seeking therapy for the effects of incest. *Psychotherapy: Theory, Research, and Practice, 20*(4), 503-514.

van der Kolk, B. A. (1987). *Psychological trauma.* Washington: American Psychiatric Press, Inc.

van der Kolk, B. A., Perry, J. C., & Herman, J. L. (1991). Childhood origins of self-destructive behavior. *American Journal of Psychiatry, 148,* 1665-1671.

Walker, E., Katon, W., Harrop-Griffiths, J., Holm, L., Russo, J., & Hickok, L. (1988). Relationship of chronic pelvic pain to psychiatric diagnoses and childhood sexual abuse. *American Journal of Psychiatry, 145,* 75-80.

Walker, E., Katon, W., Neraas, K., Jemelka, R., & Massoth, D. (1992). Dissociation in women with chronic pelvic pain. *American Journal of Psychiatry, 149* (4), 534-537.

Waller, E., Katon, W., Harrop-Griffiths, J., Holm, L., Russo, J., & Hickok, L. (1988). Relationship of chronic pelvic pain to psychiatric diagnosis and childhood sexual abuse. *American Journal of Psychiatry, 145,* 75-80.

Waller, G. (1992). Sexual abuse and bulimic symptoms: Do family interactions and self-esteem explain the links? *International Journal of Eating Disorders, 12*(3), 235-240.

Wheeler, I., O'Malley, K., Waldo, M., Murphy, J., & Blank, C. (1992). Participants' perceptions of therapeutic factors in groups for incest survivors. *Journal for Specialists in Group Work, 17*(2), 89-95.

Wise, M. (1989). Adult self-injury as a survival response in victim- survivors of childhood abuse. *Journal of Chemical Dependency Treatment, 3*(1), 185-201.

Wonderlich, S., Donaldson, M. A., Carson, D., Gertz, L., Staton, D., & Johnson, M. (1992, April). *Eating disturbance and incest.* Paper presented at the International Conference on Eating Disorders, New York.

Wyatt, G., Guthrie, D., & Notgrass, C. (1992). Differential effects of women's child sexual abuse and subsequent sexual revictimization. *Journal of Consulting and Clinical Psychology, 60*(2), 167-173.

Wyatt, G. E., & Newcomb, M. (1990). Internal and external mediators of women's sexual abuse in childhood. *Journal of Consulting and Clinical Psychology, 58,* 758-767.

Yalom, I. (1985). *The theory and practice of group psychotherapy* (3rd ed.). New York: Basic Books.

Yassen, J., & Glass, L. (1984). Sexual assault survivor groups: A feminist practice perspective. *Social Work, 29,* 252-257.

Young, E. B. (1990). The role of incest in relapse. *Journal of Psychoative Drugs, 22*(2), 249-258.

Zaidi, L., Knutson, J., & Mehm, J. (1989). Transgenerational patterns of abusive parenting: Analogue and clinical tests. *Aggressive Behavior, 15,* 137-152.

Index

About the Authors

Mary Ann Donaldson, MSW, LICSW, BCD, is a Clinical Social Worker at the Village Family Service Center, a private family service agency in Fargo, ND. In 1981, she began an incest treatment program that continues to provide individual and group therapy for incest survivors. She has published research on her work with incest survivors and is a member of the Clinical Faculty in the Department of Psychiatry at the University of North Dakota Medical School.

Susan Cordes-Green, MS, LP, LPC, has worked with incest survivors at the Village Family Service Center since 1986. She is a part-time member of the Faculty of the Department of Psychology at Concordia College, Moorhead, MN.

Together, Donaldson and Cordes-Green have written client aid materials for adult incest survivors. They also present workshops on issues related to the treatment of adult incest survivors.